HOW TO
GET MOTIVATED
& STAY POSITIVE
During Tough Times

HOW TO
GET MOTIVATED
& STAY POSITIVE

During Tough Times

YOUR STRATEGY
FOR MANAGING
ADVERSITY

SHAWN & RACHAEL DOYLE

Published and distributed by:

SOUND WISDOM
P.O. Box 310
Shippensburg, PA 17257-0310
717-530-2122

info@soundwisdom.com

www.soundwisdom.com

Cover design by: Susan Mooney Dolderer of SMGraphicArts.com

ACTivate your ACTions work sheets designed by: Susan Mooney Dolderer of SM GraphicArts.com

ISBN 13 TP: 978-1-64095-531-8

ISBN 13 eBook: 978-1-64095-532-5

For Worldwide Distribution, Printed in the U.S.A.

1 2024

DEDICATION

When seeking examples of truly motivated and inspirational people, we were fortunate in not having to look too far. This inspirational couple lights up the room wherever they go with their positive energy, their sincere kindness, compassion, and thoughtfulness, topped off with remarkable senses of humor and gratitude for all life has to offer. They have been our source of inspiration for many years now. We thank you, Jacqueline and Barry Gray, and your amazing therapy dog, Kayla.

DEDICATION

CONTENTS

CHAPTER 1

THE HISTORY OF TOUGH TIMES

"I think I am a walking testimony that you can have scars. You can go through turbulent times and still have victory in your life."
—Natalie Cole

Welcome to a life of unparalleled amazing happiness. *Welcome to—whaaat?* you may be saying to yourself right now. Yes, let's repeat—welcome to a life of unparalleled amazing happiness. If you want to live a happy and fulfilled life, you first must decide you are going to be happy *despite* what is going on around us or happening to us or in the world.

Allow us to introduce ourselves. We are Shawn and Rachael Doyle, and we own a training and development company—Shawn Doyle Training. Shawn is the CEO and Rachael is the COO. We are both lifelong learners and have always been fascinated by and have studied human motivation and self-improvement all our lives. As lifelong learners, we wanted to share with you how to get and stay motivated during tough times. (And guess what? There will always be tough times!)

Shawn was speaking at a conference and delivering his keynote, "Jumpstart Your Motivation," on how to get and stay motivated. After the program, one person in the audience asked us with great sincerity, "So, I have a question. I understand all this motivational stuff—I really get it. But how can you possibly tell people that they can stay motivated during times like these? We have war, violence, crime, the economy and political discord, riots and, well, just watch the news. Every day it's getting worse!" You could see in their body language them getting tense just describing it.

We both nod our heads and smile and say, "It's possible." Not easy, not simple, but possible—it can be done! After all, we own a training and development company where we teach, train, and coach people how to get and stay motivated, how to lead, how to sell, how to be productive, and over 100 other programs.

Want proof it's possible to stay positive during really tough times? Let's look at the example of the beautiful singer Nightbirde (full name Jane Marczewski). In case you don't know who she is, she is the singer who caught the attention of America after delivering an amazing, poignant singing audition on *America's Got Talent*. She performed an original song called "It's OK." She told the judges she was battling cancer that had spread to her lungs, spine, and liver. She impressed everyone with her positivity and amazing spirit. *"You can't wait until life isn't hard anymore before you decide to be happy,"* she told the judges and the audience. This was a remarkable woman who had a 2 percent chance of living! Wow.

In this book we are going to answer the *big* question, the one we get asked over and over repeatedly—how do you stay motivated during turbulent times? It's a legitimate question and one that is very logical. How can you stay positive when Rome is burning? In the middle of the storm of adversity? How can you stay positive in "times like these"? As Paul Harvey once said, "In times like these, it helps to recall that there have always been times like these."

Here is something transformational to think about. Unfortunately, all our lives we think we have been misled. From a young age, we have watched movies, TV shows, and read fairy tales where the ending was always "and they lived happily ever after." Sleeping Beauty will wake up, Forrest Gump will be triumphant, Dorothy in *The Wizard of Oz* will make it home, Meryl Streep will always win the Oscar, Taylor Swift will always have a new number-one song, Charlie will end up owning the mysterious and magical chocolate factory, quarterback Patrick Mahomes of the Kansas City Chiefs will throw yet another touchdown pass. In many ways we have a cultural fantasy expectation, a designed paradigm where everything will go well and end positively. In a way we are conditioned that everything will go well. There is always a happy ending, right? Wrong! Surprise—unfortunately, we are sorry, but life doesn't always work out the way we want it to. Life has good times and bad, and we can't have a front without a back, a yin without a yang.

As optimistic as we are, the reality is sometimes things go wrong, very wrong. As Rachael often says, "Believe in the best outcome but always have a plan B!"

Here are some sobering examples that sometimes things can go wrong:

- Every year in the world, according to statistics, 67.1 million people die. Yes, some die at a ripe old age, but some die tragically and suddenly from illness, fires, and car crashes.

- Every year there are over 40 million weddings in the world. We go to weddings and see people in love and marrying their soulmate and nothing will ever go wrong. Then years later they get divorced. According to statistics, 37 percent of marriages end in divorce. Everyone knows at least one couple who has gotten divorced. Everyone knows someone who has gotten divorced twice! Everyone also knows one couple who should get divorced today!

- And 40 percent of people get fired at least once in their lifetime. Years ago, I got a shocking phone call from my dad, Jack, and he said he had been fired. At the company my dad worked for in sales, he was a superstar, award winner, quota buster, the champ of selling. He was there for over twenty years—until they hired a new national director of sales. There was a new sheriff in town and he brought his own posse with him. My dad was gone in three months. Fired, severed, canned, let go, downsized, rightsized, or as they say in England, he "had been made redundant." (Isn't that a terrible phrase?) There is no way Jack the superstar should have been fired, but he was. We can't change the ending to that story.

Our point, my dear friends, is not to depress you with these statistics. But hopefully, you get our main thesis: tragedies, mistakes, and mishaps will happen and do happen. We know it is sad, but it is also true. So, if they will happen, what will you do?

If we think about Nelson Mandela, Abe Lincoln, Harriet Tubman, Hellen Keller, Gandhi, they all faced tremendous adversity in their life and still were able to be happy and successful. The point of this book is to help you figure out how to get and stay motivated *despite negative events* that will happen to you and in the world.

We are going to share with you the many challenges people have with adversity and some of ours (we have had our fair share of adversity). We will share with you some valuable tools, tips, and techniques we have used to stay positive that will help you stay positive despite the dark days you may face.

In each chapter, we will give you insightful ideas to think about and, more importantly, tools for implementing them. In each chapter you will also see something unique: **ACTivate Your ACTions Worksheets** We own a training and development company so our bias is always about taking action. These ACTivate Your ACTions are worksheets designed to help you apply the contents of that chapter to your life. There are 30 ACTivate Your ACTions worksheets in the book, so get ready to activate!

Here is what we are going to cover:

THE HISTORY OF TOUGH TIMES
THE HISTORY OF TOUGH TIMES

Chapter 2:
Your Motivational Furnace

As George Washington Carver once said: "Where there is no vision there is no hope." We are going to give you two major tools to help you: 1) mission/vision and 2) goals. We will cover the essential elements of each and how to set short-term, mid-term, and long-term goals. Goals are what carry you forward when you face adversity. This chapter has tools that will be your superhero shield to fight and survive against adversity.

Chapter 3:
Tuning Your Channels for Maximum Motivation

We will cover ways to tune your brain for maximum motivation by controlling your consumption and redirecting it to different channels. We live in an age in which we can get exposed to lots of negative, so we need to make adjustments. TV, the internet, and movies are sadly chock-full of such negative influences. A quick spin of TV networks shows any manner of violence and downright rude behavior because unfortunately that is what gets ratings. Thank goodness for good souls like Mr. Rogers, who was shining light in a dark world. As Amy Morin said: "It's difficult to look on the bright side when you're surrounded by negativity."

Chapter 4:
Challenge Your Thinking

Ernesto Bertarelli said "You can't change who you are, but you can change what you have in your head, you can refresh what you're thinking about, you can put some fresh air in your brain." We teach critical thinking in our training programs, and we have learned that many people don't ever think about how they think or even challenge their own thinking. They just accept it. We will cover reality, responses from the past, and reframing. This will help you *retrain your brain* to handle adversity more effectively. In order to survive and thrive during adversity you have to adjust your mindset. The good news is you have the power to do just that.

Chapter 5:
Learn Your Way to the Future

Good news! We live in a resource-rich world, where everything is accessible lightning fast and inexpensive, and much of it is even free. In adversity, we can seek out resources to help us heal and deal with whatever challenges we are facing. We will show you why you are not alone. It's so wonderful we have these resources available today.

Chapter 6:
Your Tools, Journals Jolts, and Justification

Every day there are tools we can use to reflect on, think about, and evaluate where we are on our adversity journey. We will guide you through using these tools to inoculate yourself against the stress of adversity and stay motivated.

Chapter 7:
Nutrition: Eating for Energy

OK, we know you have heard it a million times before—you are what you eat. A trite saying but a true one. When you are stressed, your body doesn't need flaming hot Cheetos, it needs nutrition to support your body and brain. We will provide food for thought (pun intended) and ideas for looking at your intake to create a better outcome and a better you.

Chapter 8:
The Physical: Training Plan for Motivation

We have discovered the fountain of youth and it is exercise. It's not only a fountain of youth but a stress buster. We will help you navigate your fitness plan for staying motivated all the time and in tough times. During tough times you have to take care of you!

Chapter 9:
Your Adversity Strategy

Most people only start thinking of solutions after a problem happens. What if you had a strategy in place *before* adversity happened? We will help you develop a plan B to use when things go south.

Chapter 10:
You Are the Architect of Your Own Life

We believe that you are the architect of your own life. We will help you in this chapter start to draw out your blueprint and guard against people who don't like your blueprint.

Ready to get started? Let's go!

> "Your hardest times often lead to the greatest moments of your life. Keep going. Tough situations build strong people in the end."
>
> —Roy T. Bennett

CHAPTER 2

VISIONS
AND GOALS
ARE YOUR
MOTIVATIONAL
FURNACE

" Where there is no vision, there is no hope."
—George Washington Carver

I f the idea of this book is to get and stay motivated during tough times, the question is *how* does a person stay motivated during turbulent times? We believe that one of the key elements of staying motivated despite all the crises going on around you is to have a personal and professional mission. When you get up in the morning and you're stretching and then thinking about your day, you have a mission about why you're doing what you're about to do! We believe in our company, for example, that we are making a positive difference in people's lives personally and professionally. We say, "We train; we coach; we transform." The transforming part is what gets us up in the morning!

Here's a question we would want you to ask yourself: do you have a personal and professional mission statement? We are sure you have heard about it—a mission statement is simply a written document that describes the purpose of why you are here on the planet. When you have a mission, it is the fire in the belly of the stove. It keeps you motivated and inspired every single day. More importantly (this is the key), it helps *keep you motivated* even during difficult times. Here are a few examples.

When Jim Carrey was a struggling actor and comedian, he was so poor he was living in his car. He decided to drive up to the mountains of the Hollywood Hills, pull a check out his checkbook, and write himself a check for 10 million dollars. In the memo of the check, he wrote "for acting services rendered." He kept the check in his wallet, and 10 years later was cast in the movie *Dumb and Dumber*, and his salary for that movie was (yes, you guessed it) a whopping 10 million dollars. This is a great example—although it's not labeled as such—of a mission statement, even though it's in the form of a check. That check in Jim Carrey's wallet kept him motivated and inspired through the tough times knowing that the big payday was coming. That mission was the anchor through tough times.

There is another great example in the Life is Good t-shirt company. Here is a short story from their website:

> In 1994, after five years of less-than-stellar sales and just $78 left to their names, brothers Bert and John Jacobs designed their first Life is Good t-shirt—and discovered how those three simple words could help people to focus on the good.

When you delve into the story further, you learn that when Bert and John Jacobs decided to create the Life is Good t-shirts they went to an event where they sold 48 t-shirts in that 45 minutes. This began their mission of spreading optimism throughout the world through their products. A little-known fact about the Life is Good t-shirt brand is they now contribute 10 percent of the profits back to the Life is Good kids' foundation, which helps kids going through adversities in their lives. This is a great example of the mission that is driven by passion.

Okay, so maybe you're not Bert and John Jacobs and you're not Jim Carrey, but if you can come up with a powerful mission, it will change how you are able to navigate through adversity.

We mentioned in Chapter 1 that both of us have experienced adversity in our lives. It doesn't make us experts in adversity, but it certainly gives us some lessons that we can share with you.

We don't think there's anything as devastating as losing a loved one.

Many years ago, Shawn's wife of 32 years suddenly and tragically passed away. This led to Shawn becoming a widower at the age of 54. This was shocking and, of course, overwhelming as well, being completely unexpected. Shawn as a motivational speaker and book author then had to figure out how to apply everything that he knew to his own life. After the loss of his wife, Shawn went through a healing process, and he tried to discover as many resources as possible to help him navigate the world of grief. He read books, and he joined groups. Three months after his wife passed away, he decided to take several days off and go to the beach as a retreat. The purpose of the retreat was to reflect upon his monumental loss and determine where he needed to head next in his life.

As a result of that experience and how well Shawn was able to heal and move forward in his life, our publisher suggested he should write a book about his experiences with grief. He wrote a book called *The Sun Still Rises: Thriving and Surviving after Grief and Loss.* Every week we get emails from strangers talking about how the book has had a positive impact on their ability to deal with the adversity of grief. This is tremendously gratifying for us to see that the book is making a difference. We bring this up as an example of serving our mission.

In our company, we offer executive coaching. We have a lot of interesting discussions with executives that are deep and profound. One of the questions that often comes up is when we ask executives what their mission is. Instead of answering what their mission is, they often outline what their next role is. For example, a senior vice president may say, "My goal is to be the next CEO." We then tell them that we are not asking what their goal is; we are asking what their with their mission is. This question is often quite confusing. Probably the best way to clarify this question is to say we are not asking what you want to do next; we are asking why you want to do it.

Your mission and vision statement is your *why.*

"A mission statement is not something you write over-night...But fundamentally, your mission statement becomes your constitution, the solid expression of your vision and values. It becomes the criterion by which you measure everything else in your life."

—Stephen Covey

To help you be more equipped to handle adversity, we would like you to develop your own mission and vision statement. Take the time and put in the effort and energy. Your mission and vision statement will be your compass to help you navigate through life's adversities. The truth is this is a marathon, not a sprint, so during that marathon you need to constantly be able to look back at why you're running it to begin with. It will keep you strongly motivated and on course.

See ACTivate Your ACTions Worksheet #1 at the end of this chapter to help you do just that.

The second fuel for your motivational furnace is having written goals. We are quite frankly amazed at how many people we meet across the country who do not have goals. They also don't have them in writing. Why? We have often asked people this question and the answers are very fascinating. People say they don't have goals because they don't know how to set them, they don't have time, they are afraid if they write them down and they fail they will be depressed, they've never done it before, or they think that it doesn't work.

Let's say you are walking, and you see a beautiful house. Did that house just pop up out of nowhere? No! A house does not build itself. First there had to be a dream and a vision. Then an architect created a design (based on what the owner wanted), then the contractor used the plans to construct the house. As we often say, we don't want your life to be accidental; we want you to live life on purpose. We don't want life just to happen to you.

So, if your life is a house, you must be the architect of your own life. If you don't, you will be living in someone else's house. Your goals are the blueprint that makes that happen. Goals are the buoys that keep you afloat during adversity and hardship.

Here are some stunning statistics about goals:

- In the general population, studies have shown that 83 percent of respondents don't have goals,

- 14 percent had plans but not in writing,

- and only 3 percent had written goals.

- Research has shown that you are 42 percent more likely to achieve your goals if they are written down.

If you've not done so, *now* is the time, *now* is the day to change your life by writing down your goals. We have provided for you in the back of this chapter ACTivate Your ACTions Worksheet #2 called "The Goal Tender."

Put them down in writing. Have them nearby and look at them often. They are your guide, your road map, your set point to keep you steady during tough times.

Here is a great example about setting goals. Years ago, we were at a Planet Hollywood on vacation, and we were having lunch. Shawn had left something in the car and went out to the car to get it. Walking back to the table, he found a handwritten, framed note on the wall by Bruce Lee. It was his goals written out on notebook paper. On the way out after lunch Rachael also looked at it and was fascinated by the note. We then looked into it further.

As it turns out, Bruce Lee back in 1968 was an unknown martial artist. He read the book *Think and Grow Rich* by Napolean Hill and decided to write out his goal called "My Definite Chief Aim" (Hill's term). Here is what he wrote:

My Definite Chief Aim

I, Bruce Lee, will be the first highest paid Oriental super star in the United States. In return I will give the most exciting performances and render the best of quality in the capacity of an actor. Starting 1970 I will achieve world fame and from then onward till the end of 1980 I will have in my possession $10,000,000. I will live the way I please and achieve inner harmony and happiness.

—Bruce Lee
Jan. 1969

By 1971, Bruce Lee rose to stardom in China with a starring role in the film *The Big Boss*, a film that would make him famous. The rest is history.

A sad but poignant example is written about in the groundbreaking book *Man's Search for Meaning* by Victor Frankl. In the book, Dr. Frankl looked at Nazi concentration camp victims during World War II. He was curious, comparing two men experiencing the ravages of concentration camp life who were the same age and weight, why one would die and another would live. His conclusion was stunning: the ones who lived had hopes and dreams (goals) of what they were going to do once they got out. The ones who died had no hope (they had given up) and no goals.

Here is a powerful quote that summarizes the theme of the book and ties into exactly what we are covering in this book: "Forces beyond your control can take away everything you possess except one thing—your freedom to *choose how you will respond to the situation*. You cannot control what happens to you in life, but you can always control what you will feel and do about what happens to you."

On the days when you are challenged by adversity, on the days when you're tired or sick or don't feel like doing what you need to do and should do, your mission, vision, and goals remind you why you're doing it in the first place.

> "If you're bored with life—you don't get up every morning with a burning desire to do things—you don't have enough goals."
>
> —Lou Holtz

Shawn Doyle Training

ACTivate Your ACTions #1:

VISION VICTORY

Objective: Develop a Mission Statement.

Here are a few examples of company mission statements:

▸ **Caterpillar:** "We help our customers build a better, more sustainable world."

▸ **Magic Spoon:** "To transform the cereal industry by building a new category of nutritious and flavorful cereal."

▸ **Tesla:** "Tesla's mission is to accelerate the world's transition to renewable energy."

▸ **Nordstrom:** "Our mission is to continue our dedication to providing a unique range of products, exceptional customer service, and great experiences."

Here are a few examples of personal mission statements:

▸ **Maya Angelou:** My mission in life is not merely to survive, but to thrive; and to do so with some passion, some compassion, some humor, and some style.

▸ **Oprah Winfrey:** To be a teacher. And to be known for inspiring my students to be more than they thought they could be.

▸ **Mahatma Gandhi:** I shall not fear anyone on Earth. I shall fear only God. I shall not bear ill will toward anyone. I shall not submit to injustice from anyone. I shall conquer untruth by truth. And in resisting untruth, I shall put up with all suffering.

▸ **Mother Teresa:** Spread love everywhere you go. Let no one ever come to you without leaving happier.

Your Mission Statement should be built on:

• What you believe
• What you value
• What you want to contribute
• What you want your legacy to be

List your 5 core beliefs here:

1. _____

2. _____

3. _____

4. _____

5. _____

List your 5 core values here:

1. _____

2. _____

3. _____

4. _____

5. _____

What do you want to contribute to the world?

_____

_____

_____

What do you want your legacy to be?

_____

_____

Draft Mission Statement:

My mission is to _____

_____

_____

_____

_____

_____

_____

_____

This is your mission should you choose to accept it.... And we certainly hope you do.

Shawn Doyle Training

ACTivate Your ACTions #2:

GOAL TENDER

Objective: Develop and write down your goals

Write your goals here. The only rules should be CMT: 1) Clear 2) Measurable 3) Time bound

1 YEAR	3 YEAR	5 YEAR
Professional Goals		
Financial Goals		
Personal Goals		

(CONTINUED)

1 YEAR	3 YEAR	5 YEAR
Health/Fitness Goals		

Love/Social Goals		

Write down all your goals; you can't hit a target unless you see it!

Shawn Doyle Training

ACTivate Your ACTions #3:

BIG DREAMER

We think that most people don't think big enough. They may think of a goal or idea and immediately say "that is unrealistic." The idea never has a chance to flourish. As Christopher Reeve said: "So many of our dreams at first seem impossible, then they seem improbable, and then, when we summon the will, they soon become inevitable."

Objective: Write down some big, crazy, almost impossible goals.

What is a big dream goal professionally? _____

_____

_____

_____

What is a big dream goal physically? _____

_____

_____

_____

What is a big dream goal financially? _____

_____

_____

_____

What is a big dream for your home? _____

_____

_____

_____

What is a big dream goal for travel? _____

_____

_____

_____

(CONTINUED)

What is a big dream goal for love? _____

_____

_____

What is a big dream goal for something you want to start? (i.e. a company, a charity, a movement)

_____

_____

_____

> Think big, dream big, achieve big.

CHAPTER 3

TUNING YOUR CHANNELS FOR MAXIMUM MOTIVATION

"Whatever we plant in our subconscious mind and nourish with repetition and emotion will one day become a reality."
—Earl Nightingale

We know you have heard it all your life, "You are what you eat," right? When people make these statements, they are of course referring to their dietary practices. But here is something to think about: what about what you consume mentally? What about that brain of yours? Most people never give that a scintilla of thought. We do. We are very careful about what we let into the gates of our minds, just as we are with our bodies. We know that content you consume can be confidence building or pure destruction. Let's look at something that almost everyone consumes frequently—television.

Here are some shocking facts about violence on TV:

- Children see 8,000 to 16,000 murders and more than 100,000 acts of violence by the time they finish elementary school.

- 66 percent of TV programs contain some violence, and 45 percent of shows containing violence show the perpetrator going unpunished.

- In a study of 996 TV hours, the researchers found a total of 14,821 acts of violence, averaging around 15 acts of violence per hour.

In our opinion, watching TV (generally speaking) is very bad for you. Wait, hear us out. There is, as outlined above, lots of violence. TV news is a collection of very disturbing stories with the top stories sensationalizing tragedy, fires, death, and murders. Even if it is not TV news with violent content, even if it is labeled as a reality TV show, they feature people screaming, slapping, and yelling, and fighting, and flipping tables. This is all packaged slickly by producers as entertainment (sigh). Shows like *The Real Housewives, The Bachelor, The Bachelorette, Mama June,* and *Hell's Kitchen* (just the name alone tells you something) all have conflict and horrible behavior. We are guessing that Gordan Ramsey may in real life be a nice guy, but not on the show. There is a lot of yelling and harsh criticism. It gets ratings and some people enjoy it, but it doesn't mean it's good for you. In fact, it is terrible for you and will drain your soul with enough exposure. Just like eating junk food is terrible for you, watching junk content that is violent is terrible for you mentally. It will not help you thrive during adversity.

Steve Maraboli said, "Be cautious with what you feed your mind and soul. Fuel yourself with positivity and let that fuel propel you into positive action."

Years ago, Rachael stumbled across a great TV show that featured a smart expert who would consult with a struggling business and help them turn their business around by working with them and giving them smart advice and sound business practices. She shared it with me, and I loved the show as well. We loved watching it and learning more about business. Within a short amount of time, we noticed the tone of the show shifted; it was no longer about being a successful businessperson, it was about the *drama* in the lives of the entrepreneurs and their associates. Suddenly, you're not learning about how to be a successful entrepreneur but rather watching another reality TV show with lies, family arguments, yelling, cursing, throwing objects at one another, and almost coming to blows with each other. It just became another bad reality show looking for higher ratings.

We don't even have to go back as far as Mr. Rogers, the kind soul. (He was so incredibly kind!) We can reference shows like *Ellen*, where Ellen DeGeneres used humor and positivity and shared inspirational stories of people's kindness. And when was the last time you saw someone duking it out in a brawl on Jeopardy? While we are not oblivious to the negativity and sadness there is in the world, do we really have to focus on this all day long?

Movies—dare we go there? Ugh. Ah, the plethora of choices these days. We can choose between all sorts of monsters—zombies, ax murderers, great white sharks, walking dead, killer aliens, and even a cocaine-fueled, angry grizzly bear. You can decide to fill your mind with uplifting stories such as *The Blind Side, I Can Only Imagine, The Pursuit of Happiness, Hidden Figures*, and even an old classic (which is Rachael's favorite movie of all time), *It's a Wonderful Life*. The choice is certainly yours; we just want to say choose wisely.

Oh! Let's finally get to the internet where we know everything is true! Shawn and I are dating ourselves but we used to have to go to this big public building filled with lots of books and knowledge called the library in order to do research. Now we just need to click a button. And we are in no way knocking such wonderful technology as the internet, but do we really need to post our nightly meals for all to see? Technology is there to utilize, to learn, and certainly to entertain us; we just suggest using discretion when you make your choices.

OK, Rachael and Shawn will get down off our soapbox now and get to the big point. We believe you have to follow the three Cs: be 1) cautious, 2) careful, and 3) conscious about what you consume and how it impacts your life and mind. Because it does! You probably are not even aware of it. We find that many people are not consciously aware of what they are consuming and how it affects them. We think you must become the editor of your own consumption and be careful about the voices you listen to and watch from *any channel*. We want you to take a careful look at everything that you consume in television and movies and make sure to eliminate the negative and add the positive. This will help you be much more resilient during times of adversity.

In the book *Jumpstart Your Motivation*, Shawn described a certain kind of people known as ESVs. What are ESVs? There are people who are Energy Sucking Vampires, and they surround us all. They want to drag you down with them into the abyss. When you mention any idea, they are right there to tell you why it will not work. They will discourage, criticize, demean, and limit your thinking. As Kamand Kojouri once said, "Some people are in such utter darkness that they will burn you just to see a light. Try not to take it personally." If you want to be and stay motivated, you need to eliminate the ESVs in your life wherever possible. They are not serving you well, and during adversity they will make things worse, not better. After all, ESVs love the drama. If you have some ESVs in your family, you might want to limit the amount of time you spend with them.

There is a compelling reason why—research shows that being around negative people rewires your brain to be more depressed and anxious. It's like a nefarious form of peer pressure.

As Amy Morin once said, "Spending time with negative people can be the fastest way to ruin a good mood. Their pessimistic outlooks and gloomy attitude can decrease our motivation to change the way we feel. But allowing a negative person to dictate your emotions gives them too much power in your life. Make a conscious effort to choose your attitude."

We think that life is too precious and too short to spend it with negative people.

There are people in the world we call EBCs. They are Energy Building Champions. They will be the polar opposite of ESVs—they will bring you up, not down; they will support you encourage you, love you, help you, and most of all believe in you. We have made a conscious choice in our lives to surround ourselves with friends who are EBCs. We often say we want to be around people we love and who will love us back. You too can cultivate a network of winners who have this mindset— they need you and you need them. EBCs want to be around other EBCs. They are positive thinkers. Need evidence that it is valuable? Positive thinking has positive health effects. According to the Mayo Clinic:

> Researchers continue to explore the effects of positive thinking and optimism on health. Health benefits that positive thinking may provide include:

- Increased life span

- Lower rates of depression

- Lower levels of distress and pain

- Greater resistance to illnesses

- Better psychological and physical well-being

- Better cardiovascular health and reduced risk of death from cardiovascular disease and stroke

- Reduced risk of death from cancer

- Reduced risk of death from respiratory conditions

- Reduced risk of death from infections

- Better coping skills during hardships and times of stress

Isn't that amazing? Who knew our sadness was hurting our bodies while happiness was helping it.

In addition to wonderful people, there are also resources and tools to help you remain positive during adversity, such as:

Motivation Websites

The net is chock-full of great goodies to help you maintain a positive outlook and mindset. Most of them are free. There are many great websites like TED Talks, TEDx, Goalcast, Tiny Budda, Success, Inc., and Addicted to Success. These kinds of sites feature articles and videos that can be inspiring and motivating.

Education Websites

Sites like Mindvalley, Udemy, Skillshare, and LinkedIn Learning—and Shawn Doyle Training—are a few of the many examples where you can pay to take courses on motivation, inspiration, and self-development. The sites are inexpensive and can provide a lot of great content about how to get and stay motivated.

Blogs

There are many fine blogs out there on motivation and inspiration that you can subscribe to. Les Brown, Mel Robbins, Brian Tracy, Tim Ferris, Bob Burg, and Jocko Wilnik just to name a few. What's nice about blogs is you can subscribe and automatically get them when they come out with a new one.

Podcasts

We love podcasts and there are so many good ones: Impact Theory, The Tim Ferris Show, School of Greatness, The Brendon Show, How I Built This, and Happier are some examples. When you're driving in your car or working out or mowing the lawn, you can listen to educational and positive podcasts to help you stay in the right mindset. The other nice aspect is they are easily accessed by your phone, laptop, or tablet. It's having EBCs deliver positive content to your ears on a regular basis.

We believe one of the keys for consumption is to have criteria. Criteria simply is a list of questions to help you evaluate whether you should be consuming this information or not, no matter what channel it comes from. Here are some questions to consider:

- Is the content in any way negative?

- Is the content in any way violent?

- Are people getting hurt by the content being labeled as entertainment?

- Is it helpful for you to watch or listen to this content?

- Are you learning or gaining something by consuming this content?

- Is this content helping you?

- Is it motivating or inspiring?

- Does it challenge or change your thinking in a positive way?

- Will repeated exposure to this content make you more positive or more negative?

- Will this content help you develop resilience or strength?

Please don't misinterpret what we're saying. We are not saying everything that you watch or listen to has to be content rich. We like watching a good movie or a TV drama just as much as anyone else. Sometimes an occasional cotton candy can be good. We understand that sometimes you need to watch something to just unwind and relax. What we are saying is when you watch content to unwind and relax, be careful about the content that you are consuming. If your brain is like a computer, what are you putting into the programming of your brain? We need to program it for handling adversity now and in the future. That is how resilience is built.

"At any given moment you have the power to say: This is not how the story is going to end."

—Unknown

ACTivate Your ACTions #4:

PEOPLE METER

People can have a significant impact on your life negatively or positively. Time to make some changes.

Objective: To evaluate people in your life and make objective decisions about them.

Make a list of all the people you interact with an a regular basis – professionally, personally and family. Then decide if they are positive, negative, or neutral.

People professional life	People personal life	People family	Is this person positive, negative or neutral?

Evaluate the list and make the tough decisions: which are negative people with whom you should eliminate or limit contact?

Who we associate with the most is who we become.

 **Shawn Doyle** Training

ACTivate Your ACTions #5:

READING ROSTER

Make a list of 20 books that you will read over the next year or two. The only rule is no fiction, only non-fiction. If you don't know which ones to read, go online to Amazon and do a search.

Objective: To identify a specific list of books you want to read to help you get and stay motivated.

Reading List:

Title	Author

Title	Author

To succeed you need to read!

ACTivate Your ACTions #6:

VIEWING VIEW

What you watch on TV or streaming is important for your morale.

Objective: Evaluate what you watch to determine what to keep and what to eliminate.

Programming you watch regularly:

Name of Program	Positive?	Negative?

Watch what you watch, it becomes your mindset.

Shawn Doyle Training

ACTivate Your ACTions #7:

INTERNET RETURNS

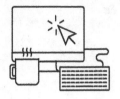

It's easy to go on the internet and get caught up in negative content.

Objective: To evaluate websites you consume and determine which ones you should eliminate.

Website	Positive?	Negative?	Eliminate?

> Everything you read on the internet is true..... NOT!

CHAPTER 4

CHALLENGING
YOUR THINKING

Elon Musk once said, "I think it's very important to have a feedback loop, where you're constantly thinking about what you've done and how you could be doing it better. I think that's the single best piece of advice: constantly think about how you could be doing things better and questioning yourself."

Although the number widely varies, the research indicates that the average person has around 6,000-plus thoughts per day. That is a lot of thinking going on! The question is, are you consciously aware of your thoughts, are you consciously monitoring your thoughts, and do you challenge your thinking? In our company we do a lot of executive coaching, and we often find people we are coaching are thinking in ways that are detrimental to their success. For example, one executive we were coaching was asked, "Do you want to be the CEO in the future?" She said, "I don't think of myself as CEO material." When we asked her why, it really opened her mind to challenge why she was thinking that way. She's clearly intelligent, articulate, and had a great deal of experience and competency and we believed she would make a great CEO. But her thought process was the opposite, and she had never challenged it.

In Chapter 3 we mentioned the example "you are what you eat," as well as you are what you expose yourself to. This is a universal truth. However, we also believe you are what you think. As Germany Kent once said, "You become what you digest into your spirit. Whatever you think about, focus on, read about, talk about, you're going to attract more of into your life. Make sure they're all positive."

This book is about how to stay positive during adversity, and a critical part of staying positive during adversity is *controlling your thinking*. You are in the driver's seat—*you* are in control, not your brain! In our opinion, there are three areas that you need to look at very carefully in terms of your thinking. They are 1) the reality of thoughts, 2) response history, and 3) framing incidents as they happen.

Let's first talk about the reality of thoughts. The reality is that your thoughts are *not real*. Your thoughts are simply the meaning that you assigned to a particular event or circumstance. Let's look at an example. We were doing training, and on the break several of the participants were talking and somehow the discussion about taking pictures came up. One woman in the group said she really did not like having her picture taken. The other people in the group were a little taken aback by her comment as this woman was by most definitions classically beautiful. When people asked why she did not like having her picture taken, she said it was because she had a big nose. Everyone in the room commented that she did not have a big nose. Why would she say that? She then described being made fun of by her brother at a young age calling her "big nose." So even as an adult this smart, intelligent woman had a belief that her nose was big based on teasing as a young child. This is the meaning that she assigned—not based in any kind of objective reality.

Jennice Vilhauer, Ph.D. said in *Psychology Today*: "Now, here is where the creating part gets really serious. Your thoughts, if you think them over and over, and assign truth to them, become beliefs. Beliefs create a cognitive lens through which you interpret the events of your world and this lens serves as a selective filter through which you sift the environment for evidence that matches up with what you believe to be true."

What we hear Dr. Vilhauer saying is very powerful—that if we think thoughts *long enough* they become beliefs. We believe you have to ask yourself what are thought processes you have that are not true? We hear people say all the time that they are not tall enough, talented enough, smart enough, good enough, or brave enough to do something in their life that they really want to do. In order to overcome adversity and thrive during adversity we have to consciously be aware of our thoughts and change our thinking.

As Dieter F. Uchtdorf once said, "It is your reaction to adversity, not the adversity itself, that determines how your life story will develop."

The big question then becomes, "How do I challenge the reality of my thinking?"

One tool that you can use, which is surprisingly extremely helpful, is journaling. Many years ago Mike Vance at Disney coined a term called "displayed thinking." We have always loved that terminology, because it is a great way to describe the value of journaling. When you write down your thoughts in a journal you are *displaying your thinking* and then, most importantly, you can challenge the thoughts by seeing them. One exercise we like is to write in your journal a positive and negative list. This is extremely helpful. Let's say, for example, you have the unfortunate experience of losing your job. Many people have had this happen at some point in their life. On the page in your journal, you would draw a line down the middle and write the negative thoughts on the left side and the corrective positive thoughts on the right side. Using losing your job as an example, you would write:

"I am very panicked because I lost my job," and then on the right side change it to, "I will get another job soon." The left-hand side you would write, "I am not sure I can get one in this area," and on the right-hand side you would rewrite, "I can get one in this area; if not, then I will move." On the left-hand side you would write, "I'm not sure I have the right skill sets," on the right of that you would write, "I'm talented and have great experience and expertise."

This simple exercise allows you to challenge your own thoughts and, more critically, correct and modify them. One of the reasons this works so well is, generally speaking, we never question our thinking. When we do this exercise in training programs, the cynics will often say, "I can't write down, 'I'm talented and have great experience and expertise'—it's not true." We understand, but our response is that the point of the exercise is to change our thinking! You have to start, or it will never change. If you tell yourself long enough that you will get that job, your brain will start to convert the belief from negative to positive. You are programming your thoughts differently. This is not some new age mumbo-jumbo; this is human psychology. See the worksheet in the back of this chapter to try this technique.

Be willing to challenge your own thinking, and as you go through the day, be consciously aware of what it is you are thinking about.

The second item to think about in terms of your thinking is your response history. What we mean by this is that it is very easy to jump into autopilot mode. This sounds something like, "When this happens I get _____ ." You may say to yourself, "When someone criticizes me, I get angry and I immediately get defensive." This is what we refer to as an *action response model*. There is an action that you have a response to immediately. The reality is that the response is based on a history that you developed based on habits. The reality is you are in the habit of responding this way, so you don't question it. You have created a rule for yourself that says "if this, then that." The key point here is (and it's the big question), "Is that kind of response serving you well?" If not, you can change the rule. Let's say, for example, someone criticizes you and you don't get angry, and you don't get defensive. Will that change the way you react to other people? Will that change the way people react to you?

Another exercise you can do in your journal is to write down your actions and responses and see if you would like to change them. We feel that we are very fortunate because we are one of the few mammals on the planet that has the ability to change our behavior through conscious thought. Here's an example—let's say a lion is lying in the Serengeti, and he is hungry. The lion sees a herd of gazelles run by and decides to attack the gazelles. It's almost as if he can't help it—he is a lion and that's what he does by instinct. He doesn't sit back and say, "Hmmm, maybe attacking this gazelle is cruel and causes this poor gazelle pain." He just does what a lion does. He can't deny his lion-ness! What separates you from many of the mammals on our planet is you have the ability to change your behavior through conscious thought. You can deny your prior thinking or thought processes. More importantly, you have the ability to change your thinking and behaviors when you experience adversity. You have to be calm enough and alert enough to do it.

The third area to look at is how you frame incidents as they happen. There are many events that can happen in the world, and it's up to you to determine how you frame them. It's not the picture; it's the frame you put around the picture, and the good news is you are the framer. Let's say you are diagnosed with a terminal disease. How would you respond to that situation? Probably your first response—you would be very upset, maybe freak out and give up. But it doesn't have to be! Let's look at Stephen Hawking, who was diagnosed with ALS at age 21—a disease that has a life expectancy of two and half years. But Stephen Hawking lived *50 more years* with the disease that was supposed to kill him. Let that sink in for a moment. We think that one of the reasons was his way of thinking. According to Elizabeth Street:

> From the time he was diagnosed, Hawking did not let his condition stop him from achieving his goals. "I am quite often asked: 'How do you feel about having ALS?' The answer is, not a lot," Hawking said. "I try to lead as normal a life as possible, and not think about my condition, or regret the things it prevents me from doing, which are not that many." Although it would be easy to think about what this disease has cost him, Hawking chose to focus on all that he still has. His brilliant mind remained unaffected by ALS, so he could continue to enjoy the benefits of that. Hawking had 12 honorary degrees and he received multiple awards, medals, and prizes. He has even appeared on a number of television shows, including *Star Trek: The Next Generation*, *The Simpsons*, and *The Big Bang Theory*. There have been documentaries about his life and a film called *The Theory of Everything*. He also co-authored a children's book with his daughter called *George's Secret Key to the Universe* to educate young children about the universe and black holes.[1]

Remarkably, Stephen Hawking decided to *redefine his response* to the diagnosis of ALS. When you experience adversity, we want you to really reflect on your thinking and remember that you are the driver of your thoughts.

> "The world as we have created it is a *process of our thinking*. It cannot be changed without changing our thinking."
>
> —Albert Einstein

Note

1. Elizabeth Street, "Overcoming Obstacles: Stephen Hawking Defies the ALS Odds," Learning Liftoff, January 8, 2015, https://learningliftoff.com/students/inspiration-and-life-lessons/overcoming-obstacles-stephen-hawking-defies-the-als-odds.

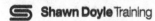 **Shawn Doyle** Training

ACTivate Your ACTions #8:

REWIRE REVIEW

It's time to think through your thinking and rewire it.

Objective: To evaluate how you normally think and to rewire those thoughts.

List 5 common thoughts you have frequently (example: I am a procrastinator).

Thought	Is that based on reality?	Is this based on history?	How can you reframe it?

Time to retrain your brain!

ACTivate Your ACTions #9:

TWO STEP

Write down 10 negative thoughts you often have about yourself. Then create a positive version of it in the next column. You may say "I am not very good working with technology" in the next column change it to "I am getting better at it every day".

Objective: To evaluate negative thoughts and change them to positive ones.

10 Negative Thoughts

Negative Thought	Positive Revised Thought

Rewrite your ending with a new positive story.

ACTivate Your ACTions #10:

THOUGHTS ARE THINGS

We once read a book several years ago by Prentice Mulford called *Thoughts Are Things*. It was an amazing book written in 1898. What you think about is what you get in life!

Objective: To look at how negative thinking can create negative results.

Write down the 10 most common negative thoughts you have. Based on the thought write down the results of that negative thought.

Negative Thought	Possible negative results of that thought or thinking

> Thoughts become your destiny.

Shawn Doyle Training

ACTivate Your ACTions #11:

WHY BUY IN?

When we analyze how we think and how changing our thinking can benefit us, it is very motivating.

Objective: To analyze how changing our thinking can benefit us.

Write down the 10 most common negative thoughts you often have.

Negative Thought	The Buy In—How changing it will benefit you

Change a thought, change your mind, change your life.

CHAPTER 5

LEARN YOUR WAY TO THE FUTURE

"One hour per day of study in your chosen field is all it takes. One hour per day of study will put you at the top of your field within three years. Within five years you'll be a national authority. In seven years, you can be one of the best people in the world at what you do." —Earl Nightingale

We are very fortunate today—everything has changed since the world of our grandparents. We live in a resource-rich world. We carry computers around in our hands (phones) and even more powerful technology close at hand (iPads and laptops) and powerful networks we can tap into almost anywhere.

Now we can find information at the touch of a button lightning fast. A quick search on Google for "managing adversity" gets **33,100,000** results (in 0.55 seconds) That is 33 million-plus results. When looking over the search results, there are websites, videos, coaches, foundations, churches, white papers, podcasts, articles, groups, training programs, and most of these resources are, yep, completely free.

No matter what challenge you have, there are resources ready to help you. You could put in a search for any kind of adversity—marriage and relationship issues, grief, financial problems, health troubles, addiction, legal situations, unemployment, or any other adversity you face—and the cavalry will be galloping onto your screen to save the day. Isn't that great? We take that for granted.

Here is the big lesson—someone has already had your challenge. Someone has lived it, experienced it, and figured out a way to thrive in spite of it. You don't need to struggle alone; utilize the experience of people who have come before you, learn from their foresight. It's like climbing Mt. Everest—you need a sherpa, someone who has already climbed it and can show you the path. Find your sherpa.

In our mind there are two kinds of resources: 1) virtual and 2) in person. Let's look at these two categories and figure out what works best for you.

Virtual

Online Groups

On the internet there are all kinds of groups you can join and most of them are free or ask a very nominal fee. Research has shown that people who belong to support groups are much more successful in navigating adversity than those who try to do it alone. They include virtual groups, one-on-one chat, online public discussion, and private online forums. Some examples of these can be Facebook groups, nonprofit groups, association groups, faith-based groups, and groups run by hospital or health systems. No matter what your adversity, there are hundreds of groups to pick from. The great advantage to a group is you have a shared experience, and you can learn from people who are further along in the journey and can help you. The key is to find a group that works best for you. Try a group and ask yourself:

- Do I feel comfortable there?

- Do I have chemistry with the people in the group?

- Do I like how the meetings are structured (formal or informal)?

- Does the group offer resources that are useful?

- Do I think the group can help me?

Websites

There two different kinds of websites: 1) general websites and 2) learning websites (our label).

On general websites, like websites for companies, nonprofits, and associations, there may be valuable articles, videos, and downloadable resources. For example, the American Lung Association has tons of resources about lung health.

On learning websites, there is a huge archive of video resources on chosen topics and all searchable! Here are some great examples of learning sites:

TED Talks

On TED Talks, speakers, researchers, experts, and authors get on stage and talk about their areas of expertise for around 14-17 minutes. Here is how they describe TED: "TED began in 1984 as a conference where Technology, Entertainment, and

Design converged, but today it spans a multitude of world-wide communities and initiatives exploring everything from science and business to education, arts, and global issues." The experts are world class, the video quality is great, and did we mention it's free? Go to TED.com and search the archive by title. For example, when we searched "adversity" there were over 20 talks on that topic alone. We loved the talk by Carrie Koh on "Four Choices to Overcome Adversity." It was so fascinating! There are thousands of talks on the site.

TEDx

This is also a great site for videos of speakers on amazing topics. How is it different from TED? Here is what the site says about it: "TEDx is a grassroots initiative, created in the spirit of TED's overall mission to research and discover 'ideas worth spreading.' TEDx brings the spirit of TED to local communities around the globe through TEDx events. These events are organized by passionate individuals who seek to uncover new ideas and to share the latest research in their local areas that spark conversations in their communities." Go to TEDx.com and search by archive.

YouTube

Poor YouTube is often overlooked as a learning site. Many people think of YouTube as a site for cute bunny videos or silly prank videos. But the reality is it is a rich resource for video learning. A quick search on the topic of managing stress reveals everything from short videos (two to three minutes) to longer-form videos of over an hour and videos by professional speakers, book authors, celebrities, and Indian gurus. Go to YouTube.com and search for your topic. The other advantage of this approach is you may find additional resources, like books, websites, or experts you didn't know about that you can tap into. If you find a resource that you like, you can also subscribe to an individual's YouTube channel to get updates every time they have a new video posted. For example, Impact Theory by Tom Bilyeu is a great YouTube channel we like. He interviews experts, and it's very informative, inspiring, and motivating. There are over 1,000 videos on his YouTube channel.

LinkedIn

If you are a premium member of LinkedIn, you can access LinkedIn Learning, a resource many people are not aware of at all. There are over fifteen thousand courses on a wide array of topics. They are high quality and taught by experts in their field. They are included with your membership.

Shawn Doyle Training

And don't forget our favorite learning site, Shawn Doyle Training. We have all sorts of articles, videos, online learning programs, white papers, and other resources that can be valuable for learning.

Mindvalley

This site is a collection of in-depth training programs by subject matter experts on many fascinating topics subjects. You can take courses individually or pay for annual membership. Take a look at Mindvalley.com.

Bookshare

This site is a wonderful resource, and here is how it is described on the site. "Bookshare makes reading easier. People with dyslexia, blindness, cerebral palsy, and other reading barriers can customize their experience to suit their learning style and find virtually any book they need for school, work, or the joy of reading." This gives access to people who maybe could not have accessed books before.

There are many other sites like Udemy, Skillshare, Khan Academy, and Coursera to name a few more. They are all fee-based.

So, it is all there for you for the taking!

Podcasts

Podcasts are also a source for incredible learning. You can also listen to podcasts when you are mowing your lawn or walking or on your elliptical or commuting. Most podcasts last 30 to 45 minutes. On any marketplace where podcasts are featured, you can search by topic.

Audiobooks

Another source of great wisdom is audiobooks. Rachael is a big fan of Audible and listens to thirty minutes of some motivation or self-improvement book every day. Search any site for books and almost all are available in audio.

The only potential downside with audiobooks and podcasts is that if you are multi-tasking you may not learn as much, and you can't take notes. But you have to decide how you learn best.

In Person

Personal Coach

There are specially trained and very skilled experts known as life coaches and executive coaches. Life coaches generally focus on life issues outside of work, while executive coaches focus more on work issues. They have been certified by going through a structured process. Shawn is a Registered Corporate Coach (RCC) and Rachael is going through her Life Coach certification process now. The coach will work with a client one on one, sitting with them in the same space or live via video technology. Coaches have experience, expertise, and many objective tools they can use to assist you. The coaching process is normally three to six months, meeting twice a month, virtually or in person. The advantage of a coach is they have an outside objective view. They can often help you see what you are not seeing. They can also prescribe resources and tools to help you. The other advantage is a coach will hold you accountable to take action.

Support Groups

You can join support groups in your local area. They meet on a regular basis. These groups are often sponsored by a church (our church has a grief group), health system, nonprofit, or association (like the American Cancer Society). Usually these groups have a trained facilitator who leads the group through discussion. Sometimes these groups also have a hybrid model of online and in person. Search for groups online in your area and find out when and where they meet. Support groups have been proven to be highly effective to help people through adversity. For example, people who have cancer and join support groups have higher survival rates. Just knowing that other people have your challenges or difficulties can be very helpful and reassuring.

Mentor

A mentor can be an amazing guide for you, especially during adversity. The dictionary defines *mentor* as "an experienced and trusted adviser." A mentor can bring calm and logic during chaos. Where did the word *mentor* come from? According to Greek mythology, during the ten-year Trojan War, Odysseus, the king of Ithica, left his wife Penelope and his son Telemachus to lead his army. He placed Telemachus under the care of a guardian who was called—you guessed it—*Mentor*, whose job it was to protect and guide him. During adversity, try to find a mentor. Here are some guidelines:

- Find a mentor who has experience.

- Find a mentor who cares about you in some way.

- Find a mentor who is smart and successful.

Where do you look for a mentor? There are many places you can look:

- **The clergy**: Your church or temple can be a good place to find a mentor. The clergy don't just do weddings and funerals. They also talk with families before and after a loved one passes away. They are on hand when tragedy strikes. Clergy members are experts at helping people during adversity.

- **At work**: If there is someone you like and admire, you could ask them to mentor you. They can mentor you professionally, but the discussion could also wash over into personal challenges as well.

- **Family**: You may be fortunate enough to have a great, wise family member, who is also positive and reassuring. Rachael comes from a family with a long line of entrepreneurs. Rachael's grandfather was a mentor to her growing up because Rachael was always interested in business. He was a great businessman. He became a great mentor to her and taught her many business and life lessons. She still uses his lessons today as the COO of Shawn Doyle

Training. We are so glad we can use his wisdom; it's one of his legacies.

- **Associations**: People who join professional
  associations are often sharp and lifelong learners. Go to association meetings and network
  with others. Find out who would be suited to be
  your mentor. If other people are already in your
  industry, then they understand your unique
  challenges.

- **LinkedIn**: Search your LinkedIn network—that
  what it's for—to find resources and people. Go
  through your LinkedIn connections and see if
  anyone might be a good possible mentor.

Therapists and Psychiatrists

Even today there seems to be a stigma around going to a ther-
apist, but there shouldn't be. If you broke an ankle, you would
see a doctor. If you have an issue, there is nothing wrong with
seeking out professional help.

"Research shows that you begin learning in the womb and go right on learning until the moment you pass on. Your brain has a capacity for learning that is virtually limitless, which makes every human a potential genius."

—Michael J. Gelb

Shawn Doyle Training

ACTivate Your ACTions #12:

RESEARCH RODEO

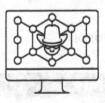

We live in a resource-rich world. Today information and support are so much easier to find.

Objective: Find information and resources for your problem or challenge/adversity.

Take out your phone and set the timer for one hour. This is a technique Rachael uses all the time and it works great! Go on an internet browser and put in a search term for your issue. For example, let's say you have lost your job. You type in the search box resources for people who have lost a job. Write down all the sources of information that look valuable to you.

Search Topic:		
Resource	Website address or contact information	Actions to take to use this resource

(CONTINUED)

Search Topic:		
Resource	Website address or contact information	Actions to take to use this resource

> A vast array of knowledge is available at your fingertips.... Utilize it!

 **Shawn Doyle** Training

ACTivate Your ACTions #13:

TIME BUDGET

Most people tell us that they would like to do something (like write a book) but their challenge is they don't have time.

Objective: The objective of this page is to make time, by setting up a time budget. Most people don't budget time, they just spend it freely. The idea is to carve out time to work through your adversity.

On the chart below calculate how much you spend in a typical day on various activities:

STEP ONE:

Activity	# of hours	Notes
Meals		
Cleaning up/housework		
Sleeping		
Work		
Grooming		
Exercise		
Commuting (if applicable)		
Childcare		
Social activity		
Internet		
TV		

STEP ONE: (CONTINUED)

Activity	# of hours	Notes
Phone calls		
Texting		

STEP TWO:

How many hours will you budget each week to work on your issues? _____

Is there an activity you have to give up to do it? _____

Will you make the time? _____

Time is precious, don't waste it!

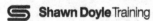
ACTivate Your ACTions #14:

LEARNING PLAN

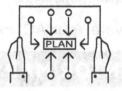

We meet people all the time who ask us how to do something. They may ask, "I am a single, divorced mom and would like to find love again, what do I do?" or "I would like to change careers, how can I make that happen?"

Objective: To create a learning plan to help you navigate your way through adversity.

Problem or Challenge:		
What do you need to learn to work around or through this adversity?	Resource	Date to start
1.		
2.		
3.		
4.		
5.		
6.		
7.		
8.		
9.		

People spend months planning a vacation but no time planning their life.

Shawn Doyle Training

ACTivate Your ACTions #15:

MENTOR MAP

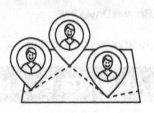

A mentor can be your trusted guide through adversity and tough times. Shawn's Uncle Scott in California was a great mentor to Shawn as he was going through grief after losing his wife.

Objective: To find a mentor to help you through your journey.

Review the form below and write in some possible mentors.

Category	Name	Why
Family: who in your family would be a great mentor?		
Work: who at work would be a great mentor?		
Socially: who do you know socially who would be a great mentor?		
Groups: who do you know in a group who would be a great mentor?		
Church: who do you know in the clergy that would be a great mentor?		
LinkedIn: who do you know on LinkedIn who would be a great mentor?		
Community: who do you know in your community who would be a great mentor		
Referral: who do you know who could refer you to a great mentor?		

Avoid making the same mistake twice, get a mentor.

CHAPTER 6

YOUR TOOLS: JOURNALS JOLTS AND JUSTIFICATION

I n this chapter we are going to cover using tools to help you overcome adversity. One of our training programs at Shawn Doyle Training is called "Pivot and Prosper: How to Use Creativity and Critical Thinking to Thrive During Adversity." Quite a title, isn't it! It's one of our most popular programs. We have taught this program hundreds of times across the world and we notice a lot of people seem to be, well, remarkably unskilled at being creative, and even more so in thinking critically. What are the differences between creative thinking and critical thinking? Creative thinking is coming up with new and innovative ways to do something differently, to think about something differently in the process of idea development. Critical thinking is more of a left-brain activity, the evaluation portion of thinking about how we think. If you can master creative thinking and critical thinking, it will help you in trying to overcome any adversity you face in your life. The reality is, if we're facing adversity, whether it is financial, relationships, health, professional, addiction, grief, or spiritual (just to name a few categories), the only way to solve the problem is to act. The only way to take action is to change your thinking. If you are going to change your thinking, you must be consciously aware of how you think.

In Chapter 4 we mentioned journaling. When you write down your thoughts in a journal, you are displaying your thinking and then, most importantly, you have the ability to challenge the thoughts by seeing them.

Usually, our thoughts just bounce around in our head, which is like an echo chamber. Once we write them down, we can actually see what it is you're thinking about. It provides clarity and focus.

Let's say you are an entrepreneur and you own your own business. (If you do, congratulations!) Let's say business is unfortunately terrible and sales and revenue are at their lowest level ever. You can certainly sit around and commiserate with your friends and family about how bad it is, or you can *take action*. Sitting around and commiserating and being miserable does not help you; in fact, it makes it worse—it builds anxiety. Journaling about your thoughts and ideas can help you come up with actions you can take to change them.

You may ask, "Why *write* in a journal? Can't I just put notes in my phone or type it on my laptop?" Nope. Research in the journal *Frontiers in Psychology* and previous studies, such as the often-cited 2014 study called "The Pen Is Mightier Than the Keyboard," shows that writing notes by hand allowed participants to *retain information better* than those who typed on a laptop, even if they wrote fewer words overall.

Studies show that when we take notes by hand, it develops a stronger conceptual understanding than by typing. Research also shows that writing ideas down improves critical thinking because there is a better connection with your brain. In the next week or sooner, make an effort to order a physical journal—hardcover, softcover—and a pen or pencil. Write down what you are thinking about.

Be willing to challenge your own thinking as you go through the day and be consciously aware of what it is you are thinking about.

Once you start the journaling process, the next step is to figure out what it all means. When you review your thoughts that have been displayed in your journal, you can then act by thinking now about what meaning you're assigning to the thoughts. Let's say, for example, you are struggling with controlling your weight. You might write in your journal, "I'm overweight. I have fallen off the wagon yet again with my diet!" You can then reflect and think about how you can modify your actions to change them. You can say to yourself, "Yes, I am overweight now, but I'm going to change that starting today and here are the three things I'm going to do to change it." Did you notice that journal entry has action? We know that when you're experiencing adversity and difficult times it is very hard to think clearly and very hard to think creatively. It's almost like your thinking is clouded. Journaling will help take the clouds away and bring you clarity, focus, and improve your thinking.

Another tool that is very helpful for dealing with adversity is something we refer to as a *jolt*. What is a jolt? A jolt is a spark or a catalyst that motivates you to take action. Back in Chapter 5, we talked about a myriad of resources to help you learn your way to the future. Any of these resources can help create a spark of an idea or of an action that can help you navigate your way through adversity. For example, as executive coaches we are often working with our clients to brainstorm a jolt they can use in order to work their way out of their problem. One client we coached was really struggling with impromptu speaking. In other words, they did a good job when faced with giving a planned formal presentation but really struggled when asked a question at a meeting and had to speak off-the-cuff. We brainstormed with them different ideas they could use to jolt their progress. One idea we provided, which addressed a big concern for them, was a formula for answering questions. We said, "Whenever you answer a question in a meeting, pause, think about what you want to say, and consider the three main points you would make in your answer." We told them to restrict their answer only to those three points. This formula was a tremendous breakthrough for them. That idea was the jolt for this executive.

Our point of sharing this example is that when you are facing any kind of adversity, the first step is to get started with solving it, and that is what a jolt can do for you. It's kind of like a kick in the seat of your pants. What do you need to do to get started on a path to solve or deal with your issue? The other nice thing about using a jolt is that once you've gotten started it gives you a feeling of optimism and hope. You have already started taking the baby steps toward solving the problem. You say to yourself, "I have a problem or an issue, but I have already started working on solving it." It has been our experience when we read a book or watch a video, that resource will often provide the first jolt we need in order to get started. As Jonah Lehrer said, "Creativity is a spark. It can be excruciating when we're rubbing two rocks together and getting nothing.

And it can be intensely satisfying when the flame catches and a new idea sweeps around the world."

The next tool or skillset to overcome adversity is to practice critical thinking. What is critical thinking? The dictionary defines it as "disciplined thinking that is clear, rational, open-minded, and informed by evidence." We think that is a pretty solid definition. As we travel around the world conducting training, we find that most people don't know how to think critically and were never taught how to think critically. In most school systems, children are taught how to memorize information and repeat it back on a test. We find that in most educational systems children are not taught how to *think*; they are taught how to memorize information and repeat it back.

The key to thinking critically is to remove emotion and to insert logic. The challenge is when you're going through tough times of any type you tend to, of course, be very emotional. You might be sad or upset or angry or defeated, so it's hard to think logically during those times. But if you practice critical thinking, we believe that can actually save you from your misery. How do you become a critical thinker? The good news is you can learn! You can use tools to improve your critical thinking. One tool that we really like for critical thinking is something called a criteria chart. Let's say you do not care for your current job; you have finally decided that you want to leave. Here's a really good critical-thinking question for when you you apply to various jobs and start getting job offers: How do I decide which company to go to work for? We think a criteria chart can be very helpful in that situation to improve the clarity of your thinking.

Below is an example of the criteria chart. Let's say you have six companies who have made you offers for the new position. (Well, if we're using an example, we might as well make it an amazing one!) The next thing we must decide is the criteria we will use to make a decision about where to go. In our criteria list we could come up with some of the following criteria: 1) salary, 2) benefits, 3) future advancement, 4) location of company, 5) remote or office work, and 6) company culture. These are just a few examples of criteria you can develop to evaluate your future employer. Using a criteria chart, you then *evaluate* each potential employer against all six criteria, giving each one a rating from one to five, with one being the lowest and five being the highest. When you are done evaluating all six criteria, you come up with a score for each company. The company with the highest score would be the one you would select. The goal of using a criteria chart is to try to make your thinking more objective and not subjective. This is a highly effective tool that works very well. When you're going through tough times, brainstorm potential solutions and then use a criteria chart to evaluate your answers.

A criteria chart can be used for any major decision, such as buying a house, selecting a school for your kid to attend, if selecting a vendor or supplier if you own a company, and even choosing who you want to spend the rest of your life with. After all, it is certainly one of the most important decisions you'll ever make. Here is an example from our personal life.

On our first date, we met at a local restaurant. After dinner, we had such a wonderful time, we decided to go to a neighborhood bookstore (being the crazy party animals that we are!). After hours of chatting, Rachael asked Shawn what it was he was looking for in a woman, and to her amazement, he already had a list of criteria! Rachael also had criteria. As we laughed and shared our criteria, we were delighted to learn that they all matched, and the rest is, as they say, history.

So our point is, this criteria stuff works!

> "Critical thinking and curiosity are the key to creativity."
>
> —Amala Akkineni

Shawn Doyle Training

ACTivate Your ACTions #16:

JOURNAL JOB

You really need to consider journaling as a way of getting through and thriving during adversity. Some people don't feel comfortable with journaling because they have never tried it.

Objective: To get comfortable with journaling.

On the chart below, try a little journaling using some of our guided questions.

How do you feel about the adversity you are facing? Write a list of emotions...	Why?
Do you feel helpless at times?	What gives you that feeling?
How do you stay on course despite the adversity?	What helps you stay more on course?
How has adversity affected your spirit?	Why?
What surprised you most about the adversity you have faced so far?	Why were you surprised?
What has been the most challenging part of adversity?	How has it affected others you know?

Congrats you have just practiced journaling!!!!

Journaling is simple, it's just thinking on paper.

Shawn Doyle Training

ACTivate Your ACTions #17:

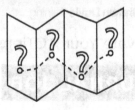

MEANING MAP

As we said in this chapter, it's important to think about what meaning is behind your thoughts. For example, if you fear public speaking and you are thinking about it, you then consider why you have the fear.

Objective: To determine the meaning behind your thoughts.

Think of negative thoughts you often have. Ask yourself what the thought is behind it. Why are you thinking about in that way?

Negative Thought	Why do you have that thought? What does that mean?

It is WISE to analyze your WHYS.

Shawn Doyle Training

ACTivate Your ACTions #18:

CRITICAL THINKING CASE

Here is a tool to help you evaluate solutions. It's called a criteria chart.

Objective: To use a criteria chart to evaluate possible solutions.

	Announcement	Timing	Topic Alignment	Technology	Consumer Appeal	History	Relationship	Totals
1								
2								
3								
4								
5								
6								

Use this tool so you won't be fooled.

Shawn Doyle Training

ACTivate Your ACTions #19:

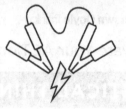

JUMPSTART JUNGLE

You need a collection of ways to stimulate your ideas for solving your problem.

Objective: Use a jumpstart to generate ideas and solutions.

Think of a problem or challenge: use the chart below to see if you can generate new or different ideas.

Resource	Ideas
TED Talk	
YouTube	
Associations	
Podcast	
White papers	
Online articles	
Books	
Google search	

Stimulate your thinking for success.

CHAPTER 7

NUTRITION: EATING FOR HEALTH, ENERGY, AND HEALING

"Our body is the only one we've been given, so we need to maintain it; we need to give it the best nutrition." —Trudie Styler

W
e are sure you did not expect to see a chapter about nutrition in a book about overcoming adversity. Well, wait until you see our new Tough Times Cookbook (just kidding).

Let's say you own a very high-end, expensive, collectable sports car (if you do, congrats), and that sports car requires a very special kind of fuel for the car to operate at the highest level possible. If you put the wrong kind of fuel in the car, the car sputters along and does not perform. If you put in the right kind of fuel, the car performs at a very high level, clicking on all cylinders. Your body is a very sophisticated machine that is a marvel of engineering. Think about this—we don't have to remind our heart to beat! (Thank God!) We have hundreds of functions in our body that just automatically happen. Focus on fueling your custom unique machine. We have learned that what you eat definitely effects how you feel (you know that already), and if during tough times you're feeling stressed or nervous or upset, you need to give your human engine the right kind of nutrition.

Jason Fale once said "Our body doesn't know how to digest these food-like products resulting in stress and weight gain. Nourish your body with real food, and it will shine for you."

OK, back to our topic. We are concerned that most people when experiencing adversity and stress will *not* pick up an apple or a carrot; instead, they will turn to junk food or, as our society often refers to it, "comfort food." Karen Salmansohn said, "Food can distract you from your pain. But food cannot take away your pain. In fact, overeating the wrong foods can create more pain."

If you are experiencing tough times, eating junk or "comfort food" will not bring you comfort; it will do the opposite and it will make your mood worse. It does not bring you comfort; the blood sugar roller coaster will bring you down. Want proof? According to research from the Cleveland Clinic, healthy foods help improve your mood and increase your level of happiness. Here's what the study had to say:

> Complex carbohydrates from whole foods (like sweet potatoes, rolled oats, beans and quinoa) can increase availability of the feel-good chemical serotonin in your brain.
>
> Protein consumption (from foods like fish, beef, chicken, turkey, tofu, beans, eggs and unsweet-ened yogurt) has been linked to higher levels of dopamine and norepinephrine, which are brain chemicals that play a role in your mood, motivation and concentration.
>
> Fruits and vegetables are high in vitamins, min-erals and antioxidants that nourish your body and have also been shown to boost happiness.[1]

So let's translate what this all means:

- Healthy complex carbohydrates = increased serotonin

- Healthy protein = increased dopamine and norepinephrine

- Fruits and vegetables = antioxidants

Let's look at serotonin. What is it? It is a chemical that is in your brain. People with low levels of serotonin tend to suffer from depression. As Cleveland Clinic describes it:

> Serotonin plays a role in many of your body's functions: Mood: Serotonin in your brain regulates your mood. It's often called your body's natural "feel good" chemical. When serotonin is at normal levels, you feel more focused, emotionally stable, happier and calmer.[2]

So, if you are struggling during adverse times, an apple is no longer an apple; it is a treatment to help you feel better, to be more focused and happier. As the old saying goes, "An apple a day keeps the doctor away." There is a reason why it was said. That is one powerful apple! How amazing is that? Karen Salmanshon said, "Eating healthy food fills your body with energy and nutrients. Imagine your cells smiling back at you and saying: 'Thank you!'"

Let's take a look at dopamine. Dopamine is a neurotransmitter. The Cleveland Clinic defines dopamine:

> Dopamine is part of your reward system. This system is designed, from an evolutionary standpoint, to reward you when you're doing the things you need to do to survive—eat, drink, compete to survive and reproduce. As humans, our brains are hard-wired to seek out behaviors that release dopamine in our reward system. When you're doing something pleasurable, your brain releases a large amount of dopamine. You feel good and you seek more of that feeling.[3]

Remember, healthy lean proteins release more of that feel-good chemical in your brain.

Whew! Now we have covered the science—but please don't miss the point of all this. The key point is this requires a shift in your mindset relating to food. The way you think about food is necessary for you to thrive during adversity. Think of food as fuel to increase your mood, happiness, energy, and positive thinking. Please don't misinterpret what we're saying—we are not perfect, and we are not angels; we like to stop and get an ice cream cone on occasion just like everybody else in the world. But if we order pizza, we order gluten-free pizza and a salad. When we are traveling on business (which is often), we are very careful about all the foods that we choose when traveling. We find particularly on the road it's easy to fall into the convenient food trap. In airports and train stations there are fewer choices. Just like anything else, you're going to have to come up with a plan for your nutrition. You notice we didn't say a diet—we said a plan for your nutrition. A diet is something you go on to lose weight and then go off when you are done. A nutritional plan is something you do all the time as a lifestyle.

There are a good zabillion nutritional plans out there that people endorse and follow. Right now in our society there is the Mediterranean Diet, the low-carb diet, Paleo, Keto, vegan, vegetarian, and many more variations of diet plans. You must take the time to decide on a nutritional plan that works for you. We are not talking necessarily about losing weight; we are talking about a nutritional plan that supports you with good nutrition in order to deal with and thrive during tough times.

Think of it like being in training to live the best life possible. If you are in training, you have the perfect nutrition in order to support your performance. In the same way, a nutritional plan is in place to make sure you can perform under adversity. There are cynics who will say they don't have any adversity so following a nutritional plan is not necessary. What they don't understand is following a nutritional plan will help prepare them for the future when they experience adversity—because ultimately everyone will have some adversity in their life—and nutrition will help prevent health issues, which also create stress, anxiety, and problems.

We once read an interesting story about the famous football player Tom Brady. Unless you have lived in a cave the last 22 years, you know he is a quarterback who was phenomenally successful but also had an incredibly long career, being a quarterback in the National Football League for an absurd amount of time. One of the things that we learned about Tom Brady was his focus on nutrition. He often talked to younger players about not eating junk food but eating nutritional food to support their bodies as professional athletes. The younger players often scoffed at his advice and said that it really didn't matter. However, we see the proof—Tom Brady is certainly a future Hall of Fame quarterback and was able to play football for 23 years. This is almost unheard of, because the average NFL career is only 3.3 years. Tom credited his longevity in the NFL to training and just as importantly to nutrition. He credits his nutrition with his longevity in the sport.

There are a few keys to making sure that you get the nutrition that you need in order to train for tough times.

1. **Have a plan**: What plan are you going to follow? Take some time to research different nutritional plans and different nutritional books and programs on the market and decide which one you think would work best for you. Once you have a plan, write it down. It makes it easier to have a strategy around your nutrition when it is in writing. About 12 years ago, Shawn was unhappy with his weight and decided he needed to get down to a

weight that he was happy with. Following a nutritional plan, he was able to lose 54 pounds and has been able to keep it off ever since. The key to his success was having a plan to follow. A plan and process can ensure your success.

2. **Shop well**: Once you have a nutritional plan, then you can make a grocery list. Plan out all the great nutritional foods you're going to buy. One of the best tips we ever read about shopping in most stores is to shop only the outside ring. In most stores, the outside ring of the store contains healthy foods—produce, meat, and dairy. The inside aisles of the grocery store normally contain highly processed unhealthy food. Go to a store with a list and stick to your list. Here's another tip—if you don't put junk food in your cart and you don't bring it home, you can't eat it, because it's not there.

3. **Plan your week**: Take the time at the end of the weekend to write out a list of meals for the weekday. On the meal plan, write down what you're going to have for breakfast, lunch, and dinner Monday through Friday. Menu planning makes it much easier to get the proper nutrition throughout the week. You also don't have to make decisions or think about it too much.

4. **Know your triggers**: Everyone we know has some sort of trigger that will cause them to want to eat poorly. Maybe it's stress, maybe it's going out to dinner with friends at a restaurant, maybe it's at work when they bring in outside food like doughnuts or pastries or pizza. When we go to see a movie, Shawn's trigger is the movie—he has to have popcorn, even if we just had dinner! It's good to know your triggers in order to avoid stepping in them and eating junk when you don't need to. We have noticed that when companies have training, they will bring in breakfast that often contains all sorts of amazingly unhealthy foods like doughnuts, muffins, and pastries. We also see companies at lunch bringing in subs and pizza. This makes it tempting for us, because the food is accessible and it's free. We dutifully pack our own snacks and will then partake of the fruit on the breakfast offering and try to do the best we can at lunch.

5. **Alternative replacements**: We have found a great technique for nutrition is to have alternative replacements. For example, instead of having a cookie we will have a caramel rice cake (50 calories and much less sugar). Instead of a candy bar we will have a protein bar. In this situation, you have to buy these items and have them around and available.

The main key to all of this is to be consciously aware of what goes into your body and to understand the deleterious effect the junk food will have in your ability to thrive and survive during tough times.

> "Your diet is a bank account. Good food choices are good investments." —Bethenny Frankel

---

Notes

1. Cleveland Clinic, "Does What You Eat Affect Your Mood?" Health Essentials, January 12, 2021, https://health.clevelandclinic.org/bad-mood-look-to-your-food.

2. Cleveland Clinic, "Serotonin," Health Library, https://my.clevelandclinic.org/health/articles/22572-serotonin.

3. Cleveland Clinic, "Dopamine," Health Library, https://my.clevelandclinic.org/health/articles/22581-dopamine.

Shawn Doyle Training

ACTivate Your ACTions #20:

FOOD FAIR

Food is fuel. We want you to fuel your tank for dealing with adversity.

Objective: To look at the foods you eat most often.

On the list below, work through a list of food you eat and why. Write down the 10 best foods you eat and the 10 worst foods you eat and why.

Best foods (healthy)	Why do you choose these?	Worst foods (unhealthy)	Why do you choose these?

You put premium fuel in your car, so put premium food in your body.

S Shawn Doyle Training

ACTivate Your ACTions #21:

THINKING ABOUT FOOD

Many people are oblivious about food choices and don't often give food much thought. More importantly, they don't think about what causes them to eat poorly.

Objective: To examine what your triggers are for eating unhealthy food.

Fill out the chart below to examine your choices.

Question	Answer	Why
What time of day are you most likely to make bad choices?		
What state of hunger are you in when you make bad food choices? (starving, mildly hungry)		
What emotional state are you in when you make bad choices? (happy, sad, glad)		
What social situations cause you to make bad choices? (a bar, a party, at the movies, with friends)		
What is your history with making bad food choices?		
Do you want to make better food choices?		

Never shop at the grocery store while hungry.

Shawn Doyle Training

ACTivate Your ACTions #22:

REPLACEMENT RECIPE FOR SUCCESS

One strategy that works well is to replace bad foods with healthy ones. For example, instead of a candy bar, you could have a protein bar. Instead a soda, you can have flavored water or tea.

Objective: To develop a replacement strategy for your top worst foods.

Write down your top 10 worst foods you eat and come up with a replacement for each.

Unhealthy Food	Replacement Food

Don't forget to drink 8 glasses of water a day.

Shawn Doyle Training

ACTivate Your ACTions #23:

THE PLAN

You can't hit a target if you don't know what it is, and you can't be successful without a plan.

Objective: To look at different nutritional approaches and start forming a plan for nutrition.

Use the chart below to start thinking it through.

Type of plan	Is this of interest to you?	Why/Where do you start
Meals		
Mediterranean		
Keto		
Vegan		
High protein/ low carb		
Paleo		
Intermittent fasting		
Low carb		
Raw food		
Pescetarian		
Ovo-Lacto		
Flexitarian		

If you don't know what any of these are, a quick search on the net will give you all you need to know, then you can start on a path to feeding your body fuel during adversity.

You plan your day, don't forget to plan your meals.

CHAPTER 8

THE PHYSICAL: TRAINING PLAN FOR MOTIVATION

"Take care of your body. It's the only place
you have to live."
—Jim Rohn

n the last chapter, we covered the importance of nutrition. In this chapter, we will cover exercise and having a training plan. As Jack LaLanne once said, "Your health account, your bank account, they're the same thing. The more you put in, the more you can take out." It's like training for an event, but the event in this case is when you have something in your life turned upside down. If you are going to survive and thrive during tough times, exercise will help you in so many ways that you can't begin to imagine.

Just what will exercise do for you? Here are the benefits of exercise according to the National Institutes of Health:

> Aerobic exercises, including jogging, swimming, cycling, walking, gardening, and dancing, have been proved to reduce anxiety and depression. These improvements in mood are proposed to be caused by exercise-induced increase in blood circulation to the brain and by an influence on the hypothalamic-pituitary-adrenal (HPA) axis and, thus, on the physiologic reactivity to stress. This physiologic influence is probably mediated by the communication of the HPA axis with several regions of the brain, including the limbic system, which controls motivation and mood; the amygdala, which generates fear in response to stress; and the hippocampus, which plays an important part in memory formation as well as in mood and motivation.

Other hypotheses that have been proposed to explain the beneficial effects of physical activity on mental health include distraction, self-efficacy, and social interaction. While structured group programs can be effective for individuals with serious mental illness, lifestyle changes that focus on the accumulation and increase of moderate-intensity activity throughout the day may be the most appropriate for most patients. Interestingly, adherence to physical activity interventions in psychiatric patients appears to be comparable to that in the general population.

Exercise improves mental health by reducing anxiety, depression, and negative mood and by improving self-esteem and cognitive function. Exercise has also been found to alleviate symptoms such as low self-esteem and social withdrawal.[1]

OK, now that you just received your medical degree, let's talk about it in layman's terms. The bottom line is, as you experience tough times of any kind exercise will help you reduce anxiety, be more positive, and have more energy, which you will need to better handle any tough times in your life. You, our friends, have to train for this fight that is coming.

We often hear people who push back on the idea of exercise. Some of their reasons are:

- "I don't like exercise."

- "I'm not an exercise person."

- "I don't have time."

- "I don't like going to the gym." (It's intimidating!)

- "I don't know how or what exercise to do."

- "I'd rather do something more enjoyable."

Let's look at each of these separately.

"I don't like exercise."

We completely understand why some people don't like exercise. (After all, it can be sweaty hard work.) But, we think that it's not that they don't like exercise. It's the opposite—they haven't found exercise *that they like*. The challenge is to then find an exercise that you like or love! For example, Shawn has always loved swimming and being around any body of water. Maybe he was dolphin in a former life! He found a workout he enjoys, and that is swimming laps at an athletic club in an indoor pool all year. Here is another example. Shawn's sister Traci started taking Shotokan Karate at the age of fifty and fell madly in love with the sport. She stuck with it and eventually became a black belt in Shotokan and Kobudo. We are very proud of her. She now teaches karate, and they call her Sensei Traci. She found it because she was willing to try.

Do an experiment over the next couple of months. Make a list of possible exercise types you might like and try them. Then monitor how you feel. If you can find an exercise you love, you will be more willing to do it consistently. Maybe going to the gym is not for you, but hiking and being out in nature would work for you. Try it and you might find you are passionate about it. Maybe it's a trampoline, riding a bike, Judo, trapeze, or Iron Man. Maybe it's joining an exercise class live or online (like a spin class) and working out with others. If you can find an exercise you love and have passion for, you will boost your energy, enthusiasm, mood, and overall health.

"I'm not an exercise person."

This is one that we always find kind of funny. What does it even mean? What is an exercise person anyway? A statement like this is really just a self-defined label. Because it is a self-defined label, you can change the definition. Maybe you haven't exercised much in your life. Maybe you have had negative experiences in school with PE class. After all, who didn't love those rad uniforms? The dodgeball to the face was so much fun! All joking aside, you can start now. Change your mindset. We get it—working out takes discipline. It can be easier (and less work) to say, "I am just going to plop down on my couch and binge-watch my favorite show." It's easy, but it's not the best recipe for helping you deal with tough times. Being a couch potato is retreating; it's not taking action!

We were inspired by Mike Harrington's story. Mike is a guy who started working out at age 69. Here is his story as written about him by Robert Roy Britt:

> Mike Harrington was a self-described couch potato until, at age 69 and 50 pounds beyond his high-school weight, he decided to start working out. Eight years later, he got serious about it. When I met him at the gym a couple of years ago, he was 81 years old and had just set an age-group world record for planking at 10 minutes. He had built up to that amazing level over a period of months, starting out with just a 34-second effort the first day.
>
> Planking, though, is a mere sideshow to Harrington's real passion.
>
> Earlier this month, at age 83, he won his sixth Arizona state powerlifting championship, setting new state age-group records for the bench press (143 pounds), squat (183 pounds), and deadlift (286 pounds) — all adding to his national and world championships from recent years.
>
> Harrington's motivation?

"I started weight training at age 77 as a measure to extend my life and improve the quality of my life," he told me after his recent win. "I consider the time and cost as an investment in my health."[2]

If Mike can do it at 77, so can you!

Become an exercise person. Why not? Here is another idea—buy some fitness magazines and read about fitness (like *Men's Health, Women's Health*) and you can then learn more about it and get into fitness mentally. Watch fitness videos, peruse fitness websites. You can be an athlete—an athlete training for life!

"I don't have time."

Got it. We know everyone is very, very busy. It is hard to schedule the time in our busy day for exercise. But that being said, there are some ways to squeeze it in.

1. Try getting up earlier and working out first thing in the morning. It's a great way to kickstart your day with energy!

2. Think about taking a workout slot at lunch or just going for a walk at lunch.

3. At the end of the workday, schedule a time to work out before dinner.

4. When traveling in airports, take the stairs rather than using moving sidewalks and elevators.

5. Fitness is so critically important that we have invested in a personal trainer who absolutely inspires, motivates, and educates us in working out in proper form. Our trainer David Berger of Progressive Fitness Coaching has been so helpful in showing us how to get a full-body workout without the use of expensive equipment or gadgets, just your own body. As David often says, "Your body is the machine!" We are so grateful for his knowledge and expertise and motivation!

"I don't like going to the gym."

Our answer is you don't have to go to a gym! As mentioned on the last page, there are many other ways to work out—the gym is just one choice. There are lots of places to exercise. There are great resources for working out with online programs you can subscribe to. These programs have expert trainers who can guide you through routines.

"I don't know how or what exercise to do."

It can be intimidating, and there is so much information out there. Here are a couple of ideas:

1. Recruit a buddy. If you have a friend who is really into fitness, ask them for help and guidance. They will be happy to guide you and be your fitness partner.

2. Hire a personal trainer. They can come to your home, consult with you online, or work out with you at your gym and show you the ropes.

3. Join a class at a gym or a YMCA. This gives you access to a professional who is teaching the fitness class.

4. Check out books you can tap into for fitness advice.

5. Look at fitness websites with articles and videos on how to work out. You will learn very quickly.

"I'd rather do something else more enjoyable."

Wouldn't we all! We all have something we do not like. But what if we could do both! On this idea we have a wonderful twist (or should we say a do-se-do) that we learned about from two wonderful creative and joyful people who are very special to us. Our cousins Jacqueline and Barry Gray are truly like our sister and brother. They decided to go out and join a square-dancing club, which is something they can do together as a couple, and to their surprise it has proven to be great exercise. It has been so much fun, and they have been fortunate enough to have met so many wonderful people. So, they made exercise social and fun!

What are the next steps?

The next steps are to come up with a plan. As Picasso once said: "Our goals can only be reached through a vehicle of a plan, in which we must fervently believe, and upon which we must vigorously act. There is no other route to success."

Here are the steps in your plan. The plan is what we call the four Ws.

1. **Why**: Identify your whys. Determine your specific goals for exercise. Is it to reduce stress? Get more energy? Battle depression? Have the outside of your body represent what's on the inside? Be a better version of you? Feel strong? Be more fit?

THE PHYSICAL: TRAINING PLAN FOR MOTIVATION

Lose weight? Look better? Be resilient during adversity? Really reflect on why you want to work out and how it will change your life personally and professionally.

2. **What**: What kind of exercise do you want to do? Marathons? CrossFit? Weight training? Boxing? Kayaking? What kind of exercise is fun for you and do you enjoy?

3. **Where**: Where will you work out? A Gym? Outside? At home? Online? With a workout buddy? In a barn? In a class? Decide what works best for you.

4. **When**: Are you a morning person or a night owl? Figure out for you the combination to the lock. When is the best time for you to work out? There is no right or wrong answer. Block that time and make it your time.

"We do not stop exercising because we grow old; we grow old because we stop exercising."

—Dr. Kenneth Cooper

Notes

1. Ashish Sharma, Vishal Madaan, and Frederick D. Petty, "Exercise for Mental Health," *The Primary Care Companion to the Journal of Clinical Psychiatry*, 2006; 8(2): 106, doi: 10.4088/pcc.v08n0208a.

2. Robert Roy Britt, "Living Proof That It's Never Too Late to Start Exercising," Medium.com, February 23, 2022, https://elemental.medium .com/living-proof-that-its-never-too-late-to-start-exercising -ce88c17cca7a.

Shawn Doyle Training

ACTivate Your ACTions #24:

EXERCISE EXECUTION

The biggest stumbling block for many people is their mindset around exercise.

Objective: To evaluate your mindset around exercise.

Look at the questions below and see how it helps your thought process.

Excuse for not working out	Why it's not true	New thought
I don't like exercise.		
I'm not an exercise person.		
I don't have time.		
I don't like going to the gym.		
I don't know how or what exercise to do.		
I rather do something else more enjoyable.		

The key to exercise is to find an exercise activity that you like.

Shawn Doyle Training

ACTivate Your ACTions #25:

EXERCISE EXAMINATION

In this tool, we will look at the 4 W's of exercise.

Objective: To determine the best path for exercise for you.

Question	Answer	Why
Why: Determine your specific goals for exercise		
What: What kind of exercise would you like doing?		
Where: Where will you work out?		
When: when will you work out?		

Apply the 4 W's to exercise and win.

Shawn Doyle Training

ACTivate Your ACTions #26:

EXERCISE BIG BOOST

This tool will help you think about exercise in a different way.

Objective: To look at and list the benefits of exercise for you.

Type of exercise	Benefit to you (physically, morale, energy, etc.)

The key to victory is envisioning winning before you start.

Shawn Doyle Training

ACTivate Your ACTions #27:

KNOW YOUR WHY

When doing anything, it is very powerful and motivating to know why you are doing it.

Objective: To think about and identify your whys.

How will exercise benefit you?	Results
How will exercise benefit you physically?	
How will exercise benefit you in terms of energy?	
How will exercise benefit you mentally?	
How will exercise benefit you for resilience?	
How will exercise benefit you for increase in confidence?	
How will exercise benefit you for stress reduction?	
How will exercise benefit you in other ways?	

Know your WHY's for exercise.

CHAPTER 9

YOUR ADVERSITY STRATEGY

"The most beautiful people we have known are those who have known defeat, known suffering, known struggle, known loss, and have found their way out of the depths. These persons have an appreciation, a sensitivity, and an understanding of life that fills them with compassion, gentleness, and a deep loving concern. Beautiful people do not just happen."
—Elisabeth Kübler-Ross

n this chapter, we will encourage you to think about having an adversity strategy. Let's say you are living life, you are happy, and everything is going well. Suddenly BAM, something happens. The question we would like to ask you here is: what are you going to do when something bad happens? As we have outlined in other chapters, things can and will go wrong. The question is, do you have a strategy for dealing with it when it does?

Let me share with you a story about my wife Rachael that many people still do not know. I must be frank here; Rachael is a very private person and I knew she'd be reluctant to ever have her story shared. I asked permission to add this into our book. After careful consideration, she agreed to share her personal tragedy in hopes of helping someone else. Rachael was the Chief Operating Officer of our company and was working late one evening on her computer when she began to see black spots. She immediately called her local eye doctor, and he arranged for her to be examined by one of the world's most renowned neuro-ophthalmologists in the country at Will's Eye Hospital in Philadelphia, which is only an hour from our home. After a series of tests, they told her that unfortunately she would lose her perfect 20/20 vision in 24 hours! When asked what the treatment was and what could be done, he said, "Nothing can be done." She had a rare genetic optic nerve issue that could not be cured. Blindness was now her life reality.

Think about this: imagine you go to the doctor and are told that you will lose your sight and nothing can be done. What would you do? As a couple we were devastated and then in a state of shock. So now what? The very next day, I was amazed. I noticed she immediately took action. Yes, action was her solace. Not allowing this adversity to change who she was and who she wanted to be, Rachael started making phone calls right away to organizations for the blind and visually impaired. To make matters worse, this was unfortunately during the height of the COVID pandemic, so many people were not available or were working from home without the use of many resources. Her determination was relentless to not allow this to define who she was.

She immediately found a coach/trainer to teach her to learn to use her computer and another coach to teach her how to use voiceover, a program automatically installed into the iPhone for people who are blind and visually impaired. She trained four hours a day relentlessly for the next two years while continuing to work as the Chief Operating Officer of our company. When asked by one of her coaches, "Just when did you lose your vision?" she told him about two weeks ago. He was quite shocked and said, "Most people right now would be curled up in a ball crying on the floor." Now let's be real here—she's had incredibly difficult times and there still are tough times, but she is still determined not to let low vision or blindness defeat her. And how proud I am of her that she refused to give up!

What did we learn from Rachael's adversity?

1. Action: When adversity happens, you eventually have to take action. We learned that taking action gave us hope. We then had resources for Rachael to be functional on a personal level in day-to-day life and to go to work again. Responding to voice-mails and emails and all the work responsibilities all had to be relearned. Heck, she even had to relearn how to apply makeup.

2. Attitude: One of the elements of this journey is Rachael chose an attitude to continually move forward to improve each and every day.

3. Accommodation: Rachael learned there were a great many wonderful, empathetic people willing to help her, but unfortunately also a great many people who still do not know that while she does not see her heart still does. Some people, when they learn that Rachael is low vision, start to shout as if her hearing is bad or, worse, stop talking directly to her and start talking to me as if she were incapable of communicating the same as sighted people. Rachael has always treated these people kindly because she realizes they may lack awareness and it is not intentional.

As a motivational speaker for over 30 years, I must say that I've been inspired by watching my wife Rachael's resilience, determination, and courage, and I'm proud to call her my wife.

We believe that to deal with adversity you have to really think about what your strategy will be once adversity happens.

Let's start out with a very simple example. Let's say you had a bad day. Everything at work went terribly, and your boss reprimanded you for something that wasn't your fault. It is pouring rain outside and you get soaking wet. To top it all off, you get home and go to start the dishwasher and it won't work because it's broken. You mumble to yourself, "OK, is there anything else?" We recommend that you have a prescription that you write in advance for adversity—what you will do when you have a bad day. What would bring you out of your bad mood? What would bring you out of your funk? What would help you? We recommend identifying what it is that brings you joy. For example, for her entire adult life, Rachael, when she has had a bad day, has simply fired up the DVD player and watched *It's a Wonderful Life*. That always brings her back to having the proper perspective.

There are several things you can think about having for your bad-day strategy:

- **Phone a friend**: Find someone in your list of friends who is the most encouraging and motivating person you know; when you have a bad day, call them up and say, "Do you have a few minutes? I need to talk to about the day I had because today was tough." They will listen to you, provide encouragement, and help you through your bad day. If you choose the right person, at the end of the conversation you will feel much better. There's also a psychological benefit from being able to talk about your problem and being able to vent.

- **Bring joy**: Identify in advance an activity that will bring you joy and get you back to a positive, motivated mindset. Maybe it is gardening, exercising, drawing, dancing, or listening to your favorite music. The key here is to decide on the joy resource in advance and have it available when you've had a bad day.

Now that we have engineered your bad-day strategy, the question is, what do we do with having a bad week, or a bad month, or a bad year? It really comes down to the same concept—we need to have a strategy.

Your adversity strategy is made up of several steps, which we call the P.R.O.B.L.E.M. model.

P: Problem

In our first step of the adversity strategy, we try to identify the problem at hand in an objective, logical fashion, eliminating emotion if possible. Let's say that you have been laid off at work.

Most people in their lifetime, even if they are great workers, have been laid off from their job. In the case of being terminated, write down what the problem is—"I lost my job"—and the bigger problem is "loss of revenue" (it always helps to be paid). When you write down the definition of the problem, that often leads us to different ways of thinking. If we say the problem is loss of revenue and we can say, "How can we replace revenue or increase revenue?" it gets you thinking a little bit differently. You literally use a series of questions to identify the problem. This also gets you out of the reacting mode and into the solving mode, which is a place you want to be.

R: Response

Although some people get very frustrated when we say this, it is true you can choose your response. Recently while conducting a training program Shawn was talking about choosing your response. Someone in the group raised her hand and said, "If your flight is canceled and you must spend the night in Atlanta, you wouldn't be upset? I would be." Shawn said no, he would not be upset, he'd simply say to himself, "Oh well, I guess I'll be spending the night in Atlanta!" In a way, is this not simply the serenity prayer? Accepting the things you cannot control? One thing you can control in adversity is your response to it. You can be mad, or you can be proactive. You can be sad, or you can get resourceful. You can be seething, or you could be seeking. The choice of response is up to you.

O: Optimism

As outlined above, you can choose your response. Sometimes people are critical of optimists and say that they see the world through rose-colored glasses. We don't believe optimists see the world through rose-colored glasses, but they do see the world a bit differently. Something goes wrong and they say to themselves, "It could have been worse," or, "At least I have my _____ ," or, "It just wasn't meant to be anyway." We don't see optimists as unrealistic; we just see optimists choosing to process information through different lens. That lens is the lens of *hope*.

B: Belief

Belief ties in with optimism because it is tied to your thoughts about anything. If you believe that things are terrible for you, then they are. If you believe they're not going to get better, then they won't. If you believe you are a victim, then you won't have victory. So, belief drives optimism and also gives you the resilience to press on. I think a great example of this is Nelson Mandela. Nelson was put into prison by his country as he tried to fight against apartheid. He ended up spending 27 years in prison. During his time in prison, he was not angry, he was not hostile, and he even treated his captors kindly. But he always believed that he would be freed eventually. Here is what he had to say about his captivity upon being freed: "As I walked out the door toward the gate that would lead to my freedom, I knew if I didn't leave my bitterness and hatred behind, I'd still be in prison." Nelson Mandela ended up winning the Nobel Prize and becoming the president of his country.

L: Leverage

What can you use for leverage to help in your situation relating to adversity? For example, Rachael uses a piece of software for her computer that helps her communicate via email. When the software was having a problem, Rachael's coach referred her to the developer of the software who was located in England. The developer of the software called Rachael and helped her solve the problem. Most likely, Rachael would've never had the discussion with the founder and inventor of the software had she not leveraged an introduction from her coach.

E: Energy

Question for you: do you want to be around positive, energetic people? Of course, you do! In our training programs, we often asked this question of the group: "When you think about a coworker, do you want a coworker who is energetic and positive? When you think about a friend, do you want a friend who is energetic and positive? In your love interest, do you want someone who is energetic and positive?" Everyone always chooses people who are energetic and positive. During adversity, raise your energy.

M: Manage It

Adversity is not for the faint of heart. When you have adversity in your life, it is easy to let the adversity take over and manage you. We think it should be the opposite—you should manage it. We often say you can give up or you can decide to be in the driver's seat. Yes, we know there may be adversity that you have no control over; in fact, that's true in many cases. However, it doesn't mean you can't manage it as it relates to your life.

Please see the worksheet in the back of this chapter to work through a strategy plan for your adversity.

One other thought process, which is very helpful when experiencing the stress of adversity, is to remember that you've done this before. What we mean by that is you have experienced trials and tribulations in your life that you have been able to overcome. When faced with new adversity, say, "I've done this before." *I have been able to overcome adversity before, and if that's true I can do it again.*

"Difficulties and adversities viciously force all their might on us and cause us to fall apart, but they are necessary elements of individual growth and reveal our true potential. We have got to endure and overcome them, and move forward. Never lose hope. Storms make people stronger and never last forever."

—Roy T. Bennett

Shawn Doyle Training

ACTivate Your ACTions #28:

ADVERSITY CERTAINTY

You need to have an important tool in your tool kit. It's called a plan B.

Objective: Use the 3 A's for working through adversity.

Technique:	Answers	Notes
Action: what action do you need to take		
Attitude: what is your attitude		
Acceptance		

Be prepared with a plan B.

Shawn Doyle Training

ACTivate Your ACTions #29:

RESOURCE ROUNDUP

We find most people have more resources available than they realize.

Objective: To look at and write down all resources that are open to you for dealing with adversity.

What is the best resource for you?	Where or who is it?	How would it help you?
Friends		
Family		
Co-workers		
Support groups		
Therapist		
Life coach		
Online program		
Books		
Podcasts		
Articles		
Other		

> When faced with adversity, resilient people tap into their resources.

 **Shawn Doyle** Training

ACTivate Your ACTions #30:

ADVERSITY PLAN MAN

This is an exercise to help you develop an overall plan.

Objective: Develop a plan for dealing with adversity.

Adversity Issue:	Thoughts
P- Problem: what is the problem?	
R- Response: what is your response?	
O- Optimism: are you optimistic?	
B- Belief: what is your belief about this issue?	
L- Leverage: what can you use for leverage?	
E- Energy: how is your energy level?	
M- Manage it: how can you manage it?	
Other thoughts?	

If you follow our problem model, your problems will be few and far.

CHAPTER 10

YOU ARE THE ARCHITECT OF YOUR OWN LIFE

"Tomorrow is the most important thing in life. Comes into us at midnight very clean. It's perfect when it arrives and it puts itself in our hands. It hopes we've learned something from yesterday."
—John Wayne

A s we dive into the last chapter of this book, we really want you to think about a key concept that we teach in our programs at Shawn Doyle Training. It's simply this: the idea that you are the architect of your own life. Many people, when they hear the concept of being the architect of their own life, are often skeptical. They may say they did not pick where they grew up, they did not pick who their parents were, they did not pick health issues they may be experiencing (genetic ones not related to lifestyle), they did not pick the weather, they did not pick the tragedy that happened their family. We get it and agree that these are all true. There are many things in life that you did not pick.

However, since you have entered the grand adventure of this great gift called life, you have made many important choices.

- As an adult you decided whether to attend college or trade school (or not) and which one to attend.

- As an adult you may have fallen in love and decided to marry someone.

- As an adult you may have made a choice in the selection of your career.

- As an adult you may have decided to have children and build a family.

- As an adult you may have made large purchases, such as investing in a home or business.

- As an adult you may have started a business.

- You also made thousands of other small choices as well.

Keep in mind that every one of these decisions or choices—*you made them, you picked them.* Imagine a fork in the road and at the end of that fork you go right or left. In the few examples listed above, you decided in each one of those situations which fork in the road you wanted. So, whether you realize it or not, yes, you were driving in those situations deciding whether to turn left or turn right. We think this concept is best illustrated in one of our favorite poems by Robert Frost:

The Road Not Taken

Two roads diverged in a yellow wood,
And, sorry I could not travel both
And be one traveler, long I stood
And looked down one as far as I could
To where it bent in the undergrowth;

Then took the other, as just as fair,
And having perhaps the better claim,
Because it was grassy and wanted wear;
Though as for that the passing there
Had worn them really about the same.

And both that morning equally lay
In leaves no step had trodden black.
Oh, I kept the first for another day!
Yet knowing how way leads on to way,
I doubted if I should ever come back.

I shall be telling this with a sigh
Somewhere ages and ages hence:
Two roads diverged in a wood, and I—
I took the one less traveled by,
And that has made all the difference.

Read again the last line of this poem, which is "that has made all the difference." So, throughout your life you have been in the driver's seat but probably not always consciously aware of the fact that you make choices every step of the way in your life. So, first the good news—you are the architect of your own life. Now the bad news—sometimes we make mistakes. When Shawn was first out of college, he decided to pursue a career in retail management. He sent his resume to several companies and was hired by company and put into their management training program. Before long, Shawn was an assistant manager in one of their stores. After working in retail for about a year, he realized that he really did not enjoy or have a passion for retail at all. He did not like the working conditions, did not like working nights and weekends, and holidays were frankly a nightmare. It was not his passion. After working in retail for a bit, Shawn decided to put it in reverse and back up down the road and change his career. Through a series of steps, he converted from retail management into sales, which eventually led to his path in training and development. Our point in sharing this story is that you have the ability to 1) make that turn at the fork in the road, and 2) if needed, then back up and change it.

We meet people who are miserable in their jobs and never make a change. Keep in mind that deciding *not to do something* is still a decision in itself, like staying at a miserable job. We see people who are so afraid of change they will decide to remain miserable to avoid it, and they will even say, "Well, the devil that I know is better than the devil that I don't know." How can a new job be worse if the one you have now is miserable?

To be the architect of your own life (and we hate to be so blunt), you are going to have to face adversity head-on. When Rachael lost her sight, she had to admit that she was blind. When Shawn lost his beloved wife of 32 years, he had to say he was a widower because his wife died. To say or think anything less would be a form of denial. These are two examples of harsh realities, but also two examples of people who were able to face adversity head-on.

To thrive and survive during adversity, you're going to have to create a blueprint to put it all together. What does that mean exactly? First, you must have a plan, and you have to have the plan mapped out on paper, just like a blueprint.

So, using this model, B.L.U.E.P.R.I.N.T., these are the steps you can use to create a blueprint for your life in dealing with adversity.

B: Be

The first step is deciding who it is you want to be. As you are battling through adversity or have survived an adversity, the next step is to reflect upon what it is you want to do, be, and have. We have met many people in our travels who tell us stories about going through a terrible divorce. They marry someone, build a life together, and suddenly their significant other says they no longer want to be in a relationship. When you go through this, after the shock has worn off you have to really start thinking about what you want to be next. In the example we just mentioned, you will go from being a married person to being a single person when part of your identity was being someone else's spouse. Suddenly you're single; your friends and their friends change and are no longer associating with you. This is the time to pause and really reflect and ask yourself now that you've gone through adversity, what is it that you want to be now? You had an old life, but what do you want the new life to be? Asking yourself what you want to be is really defining what your goals and objectives are. You may say, "I want to be rich or famous or make a contribution to the world or write a book." Or you could also decide what you want to do in terms of your career. You may say to yourself, "I'm a lawyer now, but I really want to be an oil painter." This is an opportunity to reinvent yourself. There are no right or wrong answers in this exercise; it is just a matter of deciding who it is you want to be and what it is you want to do in "the after." That doesn't mean, by the way, that you have to wait for adversity to be over to pursue your dreams; you can start while you're still going through adversity. That will help support you and motivate you to fight through it.

L: Lost

What have you lost? Anytime we go through adversity there is usually something that we have lost. That is so hard to face because we can't undo loss. Maybe we lost part of our health; maybe we lost a relationship or marriage; maybe we lost our job or lost a battle with addiction or lost our home due to bankruptcy. One way of dealing with adversity is looking at it straight in the face and admitting what it is that you lost. After this admission, you can then say, "OK, that one is lost, but how can I still move forward despite that loss and build on what's left?"

U: Use It

How can you use adversity to help you? We were talking to a dear friend of ours the other day and she said the adversity of the loss of a family member made her appreciate life even more, and she also was going to be more aware of how she treated other people on a daily basis and was determined to be as kind as possible. This was how she was using her adversity.

You've probably all heard the saying, "What doesn't kill you makes you stronger." The underlying point is, maybe we can use adversity and say, "I survived that adversity and because of that I'm a stronger person." Rachael has a favorite saying, "If it is not fatal, it's no big deal." She will say it to people when they are very upset about something that is minor. Someone says, "Oh my gosh, my flight is delayed; this is the worst day ever!" Racheal will respond back with, "Well, is not fatal; it's no big deal" (with a smile). It often results in people changing their perspectives.

E: Execute

Execute is another way of saying "take action." One of our favorite coaching questions we ask our coaching clients repeatedly is, "When something happens, what are you going to do about it?" The response is often, "What do you mean?" Our return question is, "What are you *going to do about it?*" Many times people push back on this question (sometimes angrily) saying, "There's nothing I can do!" Our response often is, "So there's really nothing you can do at all?" When we start pushing gently and brainstorming with them, they will often come up with multiple things they can do about the situation. It's easy in adversity to get sucked into a hopeless way of thinking.

There are some cynics somewhere right now reading this book and fuming because they're thinking, "I'm sorry, Rachael and Shawn, but there certainly are situations in which there truly is nothing you can do!" On the surface that may seem true, but when you dig into it, it's not true. For a shining example, look no further than Alexandra Alex Scott. You may not know of her or know her name, but she was the founder of Alex's Lemonade Stand. It is a remarkable story about a little girl named Alex who was sadly diagnosed with childhood cancer just before her first birthday. Alex was a caring and empathetic child. At the age of four she asked her parents if she could set up a lemonade stand in the front yard, and the goal of the lemonade stand was to give money to doctors help them find a cure for cancer. Alex's brother Patrick helped her set up a lemonade stand, and believe it or not she raised $2,000 in only one day. Very quickly in her community, news spread about the little girl who was helping sick children, and this inspired many other people to start their own lemonade stands in Alex's name.

In 2004, Alex Scott sadly passed away at the age of eight. Remember, in this section we're talking about adversity and not being able to do anything. After Alex's death, her parents decided to continue the work that Alex had begun. Her parents knew that there was something that they *could do* to continue making a difference and as a legacy for Alex. So far, the Alex's Lemonade Stand Foundation for childhood cancer has raised over $250 million dollars. As they often say at the foundation, "When life hands you lemons, make lemonade!" Ask yourself a simple question: what action *can* I take?

P: People

There are two people who can help you during adversity: 1) people you know, and 2) people you don't know. There are people you know (friends, family, relatives, and associates), and somewhere in that group is someone who can probably help you during your time of adversity. They may have expertise, experience, or resources to help you through your journey. There are also people you don't know who are experts you can search out online or in person.

R: Resources

As we mentioned in Chapter 5, there are innumerable resources available to you in today's world; you just have to do your research and find out where they are. Resources could be in the form of people, products, books, groups, associations, training—just to mention a few.

I: Insight

What insight have you gained from experiencing adversity? Maybe another way of asking this question is to ask, "What have you learned from adversity?" Another might be, "What wisdom have you gained by experiencing adversity?" We often think people are so caught in the middle of living daily life we don't take the time to reflect upon what we have learned from our experience. Pay it forward and share it with others.

N: No

When you're experiencing or going through adversity, you have to also determine what you're going to say no to. What does this mean? It literally means drawing your line in the sand. It means that you will no longer do something that you don't want to do and that doesn't serve you well. This means saying no to being a victim, saying no to not being in control, saying no to being weak. Being willing to say no will give you great strength as you go through adversity.

T: Tie It Up

Tie it all up by taking the time to create a strategic plan in writing for the rest your life. Carve out time today to write out your blueprint for adversity.

> "I believe that no matter what situation in life you find yourself, there is room for you to take control of little things, which ultimately adds up to big things."
>
> —Lisa J. Shultz

ABOUT SHAWN & RACHAEL DOYLE

Shawn Doyle, CSP is a professional speaker, trainer, author, and executive coach. He is the author of 24 books, and a CSP (Certified Speaking Professional). He is the founder of Shawn Doyle Training. Shawn and has been working for over three decades in the world of personal and professional development and before starting his own company, was Vice President of Learning and Development at Comcast, and was the co-founder of Comcast's Corporate University. Some of Shawn's clients include Lockheed Martin, IBM, Disney, U.S. Marines, Comcast, ABC, U.S Army, NBC, MSNBC, Pfizer, Merrill Lynch, Kraft, and Coca- Cola.

Rachael Doyle, COO of Shawn Doyle Training is a certified life coach and author of four books. A former professional photographer and co-founder of a highly successful photography studio for many years. Rachael is an accomplished equestrian and has participated in show jumping competitions throughout the U.S. As a true friend to animals, Rachael is actively involved in several charities that help animals across the globe. In addition to being an avid reader, Racheal has a passion for lifelong learning and has an impressive library of beloved books.

THANK YOU FOR READING THIS BOOK!

If you found any of the information helpful, please take a few minutes and leave a review on the bookselling platform of your choice.

BONUS GIFT!

Don't forget to sign up to try our newsletter and grab your free personal development ebook here:

soundwisdom.com/classics